SECRETS
—OF—
MINDSHARE

REVENUE PRODUCERS
GET THE REFERRALS
THEY WANT BY
MAKING THEIR
COMPETITION
IRRELEVANT

KENNETH M. POTALIVO

ProGrowth LLC
San Juan Capistrano, CA
2014

ISBN: 978-0-9909496-0-2

ProGrowth LLC
31103 Rancho Viejo Rd.
Suite D-2240
San Juan Capistrano, CA 92675
secretsofmindshare.com

This book is meant to provide general information only. It is intended, but not promised or guaranteed, to be correct, complete, and up-to-date. Therefore, readers of this publication should seek the advice of a competent professional advisor before entering into any transaction that has tax or financial consequences.

Cover designer: Austin Rubben, 99designs
Interior designer: Lorie DeWorken, MINDtheMARGINS, LLC
Copyeditor: Dara Holland - daraholland.com

TABLE OF CONTENTS

Acknowledgements

Writing *Secrets of Mindshare* was not only an exciting adventure, but a gift made possible by all the amazing people whose lives are reflected in its pages. As a business coach, I am grateful to the many professionals who have trusted me to guide their futures. Their desire to achieve success and willingness to do the necessary work fueled my strength and passion to help them create the lives they wanted.

While my clients learned from me, I learned much more from them. Their stories, challenges, and triumphs are what brought *Secrets of Mindshare* to life. These are hardworking professionals who strive for a thriving business and a happy personal life. Without their experiences, I could not have communicated the essence of the book: learning and doing what it takes to build a strong brand and create a solid mindshare position.

I also want to thank Dara Holland, who has been an outstanding copy editor and really knows how to "polish the apple." She believes in our message and was on a mission to challenge me to communicate it clearly—to make *Secrets of Mindshare* an enjoyable, easy read, and a life-changing tool.

For the gift of many weekends and early mornings to write and edit, I thank my wife, Betty. She is an incredible partner and confidant. She has allowed me to bounce ideas and concepts off her, and I deeply appreciate her perspective and ideas.

I also owe a debt of gratitude to my wonderful daughter Missy and her firm, socialsensemarketing.com. Missy is an expert in social media and has helped give my company, ProGrowth, significant national exposure through various social media outlets.

Thanks also to my daughter Kim and her husband Chad. They are inspirational in the way they balance busy careers with a wonderful family life centered on three great children, Taylor, Gracie, and Everett.

My stepsons, Mack and Buck, deserve credit for teaching me a thing or two about life. It's been a thrill to watch them grow into young men of character—to develop so well, and remain close and loving brothers, in spite of being so different from each other.

As the son of a military officer, I learned early on the importance of relationships. Because of my father's career, our family moved frequently and spent many years living in different countries. My sister, Ginny, and brothers Bob, Larry, Charlie, and I have always depended on each other for guidance and camaraderie. Their invaluable advice and counsel have kept me grounded.

Finally, my acknowledgements would not be complete without a tribute to my mother, Ruth, who taught me so much about life and people. Mom was the most giving person I've ever met. She put everyone else's needs before her own. I watched Mom make so many sacrifices, yet never heard her complain. She always gave people the benefit of the doubt, and chose to see the good in everyone. It's an outlook I cherish to this day—and credit for driving me to want to help others.

Foreword

Mark Goulston, M.D., Author

Just Listen: Discover the Secret to Getting Through to Absolutely Anyone
Real Influence: Persuade Without Pushing and Gain Without Giving In
Get Out of Your Own Way

Ken Potalivo and I have known each other for over 15 years. I met him at an event in Los Angeles and was intrigued by the approach he takes to coaching service professionals.

We've had many discussions through the years and I have been privileged to speak at some of his ProGrowth events. The key to what Ken has been teaching for almost two decades is that we professionals are interdependent; our overall success hinges on our ability to develop a consistent flow of referrals to the right clients.

Ken's approach centers on the concept of creating highly collaborative relationships that actually cause your competition to become irrelevant. He understands the human dynamics that take place in order to get there, and has a gift for explaining the process to others. Ken's methodology is spot on because it recognizes that for any of us to get a referral from someone, we need to first find out what truly matters to that person and then have it matter to us. Our ability to gain MindShare is dependent, in part, on how well we communicate to others that we care about them and truly want to help them. It's what I refer to as letting go of "you're here" to go to "their there" and then care about them when you're there. I am also very keen on Ken's approach because in Heartfelt Leadership, the global community I co-founded, our mantra is: "Daring to Care" and *Secrets of Mindshare* is not just about connecting head to head, but heart to heart.

I am a board-certified psychiatrist and former FBI and police hostage negotiation trainer. I work daily with successful CEO's, executive teams, and senior management to accelerate their ability to resolve people problems. Most professionals believe that because they're smart and good at what they do, their phone should be ringing non-stop. Unfortunately, things aren't that simple.

In *Secrets of MindShare,* Ken will help you see that, when it comes time to giving a referral, the overwhelming reason people will choose you and not your competition is a direct result of *all* the things that affect how they "feel" about you. With potential referrers, their perception becomes your reality.

There are plenty of books out there that will tell you how you should network and the way you should act if you want to become a rainmaker for your firm. But, Ken's unique approach, which he shares completely in *MindShare,* offers a proven specific process and structure that will give you the tools you need to build and sustain a successful service business for years to come—regardless of the economic environment. I personally know many professionals who have worked with Ken, and can attest that the process he took them through changed their lives in a very positive way.

Secrets of MindShare is a great book if you're just starting out in your career, in the middle of it, or looking to make an impact in the twilight years. I hope you'll read Ken's book with care and put its principles into practice. You—and your fellow service professionals—will be glad you did.

Introduction

HOW I DISCOVERED MINDSHARE

For service professionals of all disciplines, the world has changed dramatically over the past twenty years. As the population of professionals continues to grow, the number of potential clients now declines as technological advances, mergers, bankruptcies, and other macro-economic events cause companies to shift operations—and business—across the globe. **Consequently, what was once a competitive situation is now a hyper-competitive environment.** This, in turn, has put pressure on service professionals to reduce their fees, adding further stress to their business and personal lives.

Many firms struggle to keep their people busy, while holding expenses down. In addition, long-time partners with large salaries who are bringing in little or no business are being forced to retire or resign. The law field has been particularly affected. According to an article entitled "Why It's Time for Big Law to 'Adapt or Die'" in the January 2014 issue of *Bloomberg Businessweek* magazine, law firm leaders will have no choice but to cut equity partners who are not bringing in enough business if they want to remain competitive.

More than ever, service professionals today need to know how to bring in new business.

The signs of the time are everywhere for young and veteran professionals alike. Regardless of where you work, at some point, you need to be generating business for your organization; otherwise, your career will likely suffer. If your firm's business declines, your technical skills may no longer be necessary, and you'll probably find yourself seeking a new job.

I wrote *Secrets of Mindshare* with professionals like you in mind. I know the pressure you're under to do quality work *and* bring in clients to sustain and grow the business. For almost two decades, I have coached hundreds of service professionals on that crucial but often overlooked second element: bringing in new clients. By doing so, I've helped them build predictable businesses and satisfying personal lives.

It's all about taking chance out of the equation.

Mindshare was born from a need I observed repeatedly while working and associating with various service professionals—lawyers, accountants, consultants, wealth managers, commercial and investment bankers, commercial insurance, stock and real estate brokers, and more. For nearly 20 years, I witnessed up close and personal how challenged most service professionals are in understanding how to create business. I'm talking about competent professionals, who grasp the realities of the New World order and who desperately *want* to bring business into their firms! My observations led me to believe there had to be a better way to build a reliable, predictable business that would help professionals achieve the success they wanted. Leaving things to chance, which is what most professionals do, wasn't cutting it.

Time and time again, I watched as highly educated and trained practitioners struggled to generate referrals. I knew that if they could get in front of prospective clients, and get a chance to prove their worth, they would do a great job and win new business. Yet, so many of them were failing, or having just enough success to encourage them to continue their efforts—but never reaching their new business goals.

As I began searching for answers to this challenging situation, I discovered there were ways of doing business that were unique to successful service professionals. **The more I studied these principles, the more I became convinced that the competitive advantage successful professionals had over unsuccessful professionals was the ability to gain *mindshare*. Professionals who were successful had an undeniable hold on people's attention that caused potential referral sources to call them, and not their competition.**

My path to understanding the secrets of mindshare began in 1989, in a restaurant in downtown Los Angeles. I was sitting with two service professionals who wanted access to a greater number of other service professionals who could send them referrals. We decided to develop our own networking group, a community of practitioners in various but non-competing disciplines. Our target members would be service professionals who had one thing in common: they needed to be able to get enough referrals to generate a consistent revenue stream.

We were hopeful that if enough people were involved, everyone would benefit by getting referrals to build their respective businesses and achieve their income goals. And so, our non-profit group PNG was born. I agreed to build chapter groups in Orange

County, California, while the other two professionals developed groups in Los Angeles. We decided that groups of thirty to forty members with no duplication of disciplines would serve everyone's best interest. It seemed logical that if members participated and attended their chapter meetings and a monthly "troika" with two or three other members, everyone would prosper.

Referrals would flow.

Clients would be won.

Our goal was to give members a platform to develop the business and the life they imagined when they set out to establish their careers.

During a six-year period, we built four groups in Orange County, California. They included some wonderful people I remain friends with to this day. While we saw significant growth in the number of PNG members, over time, it became apparent that many of these highly educated and knowledgeable professionals were not making progress towards growing their businesses and were not getting referrals. On the surface, this was shocking, especially given that many had acquired their technical skills at highly prestigious institutions, such as Harvard, Columbia, Yale, Stanford, USC, and most of the UC schools. There was no doubt these professionals could perform well for clients on a technical level. **So, why wasn't anyone calling them?**

What I observed working with these truly gifted and talented individuals was that, while they had invested considerably in their professional credentials, they had little or no training in ***developing the business skills*** that are necessary to build a sustainable business. A profitable service business requires a consistent flow of qualified referrals. Getting referrals requires having a strong brand in order to create a space in the mind of someone who can refer business. **These accomplished men and women—all of whom were technically strong in their respective industries—didn't have a clue how to form the relationships they needed to successfully generate business referrals.**

An Ivy League education doesn't matter when your value is summed up in two questions: "How good is your work?" and "How much business are you bringing into the firm?" Of the professionals we met with, few were able to keep their jobs simply because they had graduated from Harvard or Stanford. Even when they could, if there wasn't enough business to keep them busy, they were soon looking for the next firm that might require their technical skills.

My impression was that many PNG members had been told they needed to bring in business to be deemed valuable to their firms, and thought joining a networking group would make that happen. Not knowing what to do, they felt if they showed up for our PNG meetings and passed out a few cards that their phones would start to ring and a willing professional with a referral would be on the other end of the line.

Unfortunately, that's not how it works.

Many times, a member of one of the groups would come to me and complain they'd been in PNG for over a year and hadn't received a single referral. Not one opportunity that had led to a client. They were truly disappointed because they had presumed being a PNG member *entitled* them to referrals. Maybe even guaranteed them. They felt that being a part of the group would cause other members to call them with referrals and that the time they invested by showing up, passing out their business card, shaking hands, and saying a few pleasantries would magically generate the referrals they wanted. **I empathized with these**

members, but, at the same time, immediately understood why they were struggling.

Many of them were confused about their identity. Not their personal identity, but their professional one. The biggest problem was that many **could not clearly and simply describe what they did and who they did it for. Their brand was weak and it was obvious they lacked confidence in describing their value proposition. Weak brands are not memorable.** And, when your brand is weak, it doesn't matter where you show up or how many cards you pass out, you are not going to impress people and earn the trust needed to win referrals. So, while these members may have had many acquaintances, they had very few meaningful business relationships.

Because they lacked confidence in promoting their brand, these otherwise talented professionals simply were not memorable. And why was this the case? Because the only time they saw the people in their PNG group was at the monthly meetings and troikas they were required to attend. Even worse, one or two of their group members often didn't even work with the type of clients they each sought. In other words, many members were wasting time meeting with people who had nothing to with their industries and thus were unlikely to give or get any referrals.

Early in 1996, two simultaneous events took place that helped shape the future of everyone I'd work with over the next eighteen years. I decided to leave the corporate world and set out to buy or build my own business. Around the time I was considering possibilities, I read an article in the February issue of *Newsweek* magazine about professional coaching, a new service taking hold in the business community.

The idea struck me as if I'd been hit by lightning. It was clear that professionals of all disciplines could benefit from learning how to bring in business to their firms, but that there was little if any training available. Instinctively, I felt my skills and experience were a perfect fit for satisfying this need. I realized I could coach and teach professionals to build strong brands that could create mindshare and attract the referrals they wanted.

I was excited about starting a coaching practice to help PNG members and other professionals build sustainable businesses. I was convinced their professional lives depended on it. With my business background, psychology degree, MBA, and many successful years in the service industry, I knew I could make a positive difference in the lives of struggling service professionals. I wanted to see them realize their dreams of having a sustainable business that would provide the success and security they wanted.

I began to formulate a plan for building a structure and process that would train service professionals how to function like a business, not just a practitioner. I knew it didn't matter if they were self-employed, a partner in a firm, or part of a large organization; ultimately, people were going to do business with them because of *them*.

They would become their own brand.
And they would learn to make that brand thrive.

It was evident that service professionals who were the most successful wore both hats well: they were proficient as both business people and practitioners.

Over the next six months, I focused on developing a solution that would help professionals create self-sustaining business. At its core was brand building of the kind that rendered competition irrelevant, leading to consistent referrals.

I was excited to help people, and knew that there were many more who could benefit from my program. I put time and effort into research and over the course of that year **I developed a process and a structure that would enable service professionals of all disciplines to get the referrals they wanted.** After studying some of the most successful service professionals in every discipline, one thing had become crystal clear: **they all had the ability to create mindshare—space in someone else's mind that was reserved solely for them.** They all knew building a sustainable business wasn't about having many acquaintances; **it was about having a few meaningful relationships with people who actively worked together for their mutual benefit.** It was also clear successful service professionals were so confident about who they served best that they intentionally sought out the right people who could refer them to the right kind of clients. **Getting referrals must be intentional and dynamic.**

The practice of mindshare is built around developing highly collaborative relationships where you are in the number one mindshare position. Holding that crucial #1 spot means that when someone has a client who needs your services, they call you—never your competition. This concept takes into account all the elements of an individual's personal and professional life that cause him or her to create memorable space in another professional's brain. **That is, to create mindshare.** This is the only way you can truly make your competition irrelevant.

My plan was to develop a group of forty to fifty seasoned professionals who I could coach personally, one on one, towards building a sustainable business using the mindshare concept. **My method is based on the premise that all service professionals are businesses in every sense of the word.** I start by asking my clients to begin thinking like business owners—to reboot their brains, so to speak, and rid themselves of the typical mindset of most service professionals. For example, if I was working with an attorney, I asked her to no longer view herself as a lawyer running a "practice," but as a business owner running a business. Since her business offered a very specific legal service, she could easily define *what she does* as a product that appeals to a specific set of clients—*who she does it for* (or, who she best serves.) It could be easily communicated and understood by others.

To create mindshare effectively, every business needs absolute clarity in what they do and who they do it for. If you don't have clarity about your services, you can't expect others to have clarity about you or your business. I have found no exceptions to this rule.

This book will teach you how to carefully define these two aspects of your service. Keep in mind you must work at this. If you do the work, the benefits will be immeasurable. You'll see them in your growing client list, in the constant stream of referrals and, most importantly, in the success of your business and bank account. For almost two decades, this method has worked for hundreds of professionals, many of whom never thought they had it in them to be a rainmaker. You will learn that anyone can be a rainmaker—including you.

January 1997 found me starting my new venture, which I called ProGrowth. As you might expect, there was no grand rush of clients through my front doors. Instead, I built my practice one client at time. I was encouraged, as it quickly became apparent that professionals were thirsting for a different, more effective approach to growing their businesses. People appreciated the mindshare structure and process and realized it wasn't hocus-pocus. Yes, the system took work, but as my clients used it, they began to get undeniable results.

As for myself, by June 1997, I had a full practice of fifty professionals. I'm happy to say I know the mindshare system works, because it has changed many lives in significant ways. As a direct result of mindshare, my clients have increased their income, become esteemed partners in firms, and even developed the confidence to start their own businesses. Gaining the power of mindshare made them feel better about themselves, which had a positive impact on their families, co-workers, and clients.

Throughout those years, I've been honored to work with some of the most energetic and accomplished professionals around: people who bring value to their clients every day and, as a result, enjoy the prosperity they've always dreamed of having for themselves and their families. I feel privileged to have gone along on the ride with them, and I've learned as much from my clients as they've learned from me. (Maybe even more.)

While I still do professional coaching, I've expanded my work to include speaking, offering seminars for professionals, facilitating retreats, and implementing mindshare programs to firms of all sizes to assist their professionals in contributing to the long-term growth of their organizations.

I'm excited about what you'll learn in this book. It will equip you to change your life in a very positive way. Early on, I chose to work with talented committed professionals like you who pour their hearts out every day to help clients solve problems, create opportunities, or improve themselves. We service professionals, have unique challenges that our brethren in the corporate world do not necessarily face. We *are* the brand. We create and/or deliver the product. We must also be able to bring in business. And, we need time for our families and ourselves. Time is our most precious commodity. So, we must use it wisely and to its highest and best use. I'm certain that if you put this method into practice, you'll enjoy the life you want *and* achieve sustainable and predictable growth in your service business.

Secrets of Mindshare was written to reveal the solutions you need to build a sustainable business. It doesn't matter what service you provide. From attorneys, to dog groomers, to investment bankers, to landscapers, this book is meant for anyone who depends upon referrals. In its pages, you will discover the secrets to getting a consistent flow of the referrals you want from the right people who have the ability to refer you to the clients you want.

I've dedicated nearly two decades of my life to helping service professionals succeed. These are mainly people whose livelihoods depend on their reputations and skills—who often have few resources other than sheer determination to back them up. You'll hear some of their stories and learn from their experiences as you read through the chapters. You may even see a bit of yourself in them.

My commitment to helping people like you stems from this: I admire you for bringing value to your clients, helping them in the myriad ways you do to make their lives better. I truly want you to be the one who comes to mind when someone in your community needs the service you provide. Why shouldn't you be memorable? Why shouldn't your name and face and the ways you make people's lives better rise first in the minds of your centers of influence?

We're going to harness all these "should's," so you reap the benefits. I am absolutely committed to helping you make it happen. That's why I've written this book. After you've read it, I hope you will contact me. I'd love to hear about your progress.

PART ONE

The Importance of Mindshare

We kick off Part One by learning what mindshare means. From there, we'll delve into the brand that is *you*, and discuss the elements of your brand that compose mindshare. Then, it's on to why competent professionals fail financially and what can be done about it. Finally, we will take a look at how you can build a relationship system using strong mindshare positioning that will make your competition irrelevant.

1

WHAT IS MINDSHARE?

Mindshare—
a controlling or predominant hold of one's attention.
—*MERRIAM WEBSTER*

Back in 1984, an eerie TV ad ran just twice—but got *everyone's* attention. Perhaps you remember. It went like this:

The screen flickers in black and white hues as a line of hairless, gray-clad men with drone-like stares march single-file into a cavernous room. Big Brother's voice echoes from the screen above them, pontificating on the virtues of conformity. Everyone looks disturbingly alike, suggesting clones with their identical dress and passive expressions that convey an incapacity for independent thought. We hear the voice of a rational orthodoxy and status quo of the times. Big Brother. IBM.

Cut to a runner clad in red shorts and a white tank top carrying a sledge hammer. Her short blonde hair bounces and catches the light as she sprints down the same gray steel ramp toward the voice. She is flesh and blood, fully human, a flash of color, beauty, and strength. Security men in riot helmets and batons chase after her. She stops in the aisle between the endless rows of hypnotized clones, spins around with the hammer to gain momentum, then launches it at the screen, smashing it. The ensuing explosion blasts the clones in their seats with a hard wind of freedom, their mouths gape open in amazement, and they are forever free to think for themselves.

What image comes on the screen next? A piece of familiar red fruit with a bite taken out of it. You know the company. What do you know them for? Simply this: Its products create value in customers' lives because they make doing mundane things easy and exciting. Every time this company introduces a new product, customers and competitors alike scramble. Lines at dedicated retail stores form long before sunrise, brimming with people who are anxious to purchase history in the making.

Think of the company's first portable digital player for music; it buried the popular Walkman. Think of its first portable telephone that has become far more than a calling device. Think of a stand-alone computer that can do just about anything with graphics. It has run neck and neck with IBM-compatible PC's since its inception, and is seen as a versatile and coveted competitor.

What name comes to your mind when you think of these products?

Everything you are thinking regarding this company is what I call "mindshare." That is, the symbol of this company has created a space in your thinking that communicates its brand every time you think of the phone, music player, or personal computer it produces. This company has done two things so consistently well that its name and brand are in your mind *even if you don't use its products*. Its reputation for innovation, style, functionality, and creativity are almost unparalleled. It has the ability to shift markets, precisely because such a high degree of mindshare has entered the minds of both consumers and businesses.

You know which company I'm talking about. But do you see how the power of a brand determines the strength of mindshare in a person's memory? It bears witness to this simple fact: *mindshare works.*

What Apple Has Accomplished

Let's pin down exactly what Apple has accomplished in its branding efforts by making a few simple observations.

First, Apple has created amazing **utility** in its products. Apple's innovative functions not only bring value to the lives of users, but are known for delivering high quality and unique functionality.

Second, Apple has leveraged that utility to create certain **perceptions** in consumer's minds and hearts. It's how people *feel* about Apple products that makes its customers so rabidly loyal. From the quality of its stores to its unique packaging, everything is designed to make you feel good about being in the Apple sphere. Translation? Buy Apple, feel special.

Obviously, what Apple accomplished—and continues to promote—has not been easy. Mindshare is established based on the strength of a company or service professional's brand, which, in turn, is supported by the two pillars of *utility* and *perception.*

Granted, Apple has spent billions of marketing dollars over the last thirty years leveraging the utility of its products. The result is a universal perception that Apple is the world's leading innovator in personal computing, phones, and music. Put another way, Apple has spent a fortune getting inside your head. When a new Apple product comes out, you never wonder if it will work; you "trust" that it will, and in an amazing, user-friendly, reliable way, because the Apple brand has an envious track record for being all this and more.

A brand is nothing more than a promise. **If you're inclined to make a purchase, most of the time you will do it on reputation alone.** Apple is a clear winner in this category. The company has so successfully fueled a strong perception of reliability, style, and quality in your thinking that you won't even hesitate to shell out top dollar for anything Apple produces.

Its brand is that strong.

Service professionals must do the same thing. In this book, I'll show you what it takes to develop a system of consistent referrals using mindshare—and how you get it by building a strong brand. The secrets you will learn will significantly increase your value to your organization, help you build a long-term stable business, and make you extremely valuable in the marketplace. I know you don't have anywhere near the billions of dollars Apple has spent on creating and marketing its products. But, you can apply the same principles Apple utilizes to build worldwide mindshare to grow your own professional relationships and business. You can build *your* brand based on clarity of the *utility* of what you do and why, and, most importantly, by building a strong positive *perception* in the minds of others.

The successful service professionals in today's hyper-competitive market have influenced their relationships to the point that they are in the first or second mindshare position of a referrer. If you are in third or fourth position when a need for your service arises, chances are slim you'll get the call. **The power of your brand determines your mindshare position.**

There is an order in a referrer's mind that determines whether they will or won't refer business to you. My nearly two decades of experience coaching hundreds of clients across various disciplines tell me that people make this determination based

20% on utility, 80% on brand perception. As a service professional, everything you do publicly and privately shapes the brand known as <u>you</u>. Everything is interrelated. How you feel professionally affects how you feel personally (and visa versa) and *everything* spills over into the make-up of your brand—directly impacting the mindshare position you hold with others.

So, what do *utility* and *perception* mean, and how do they affect decisions on whether your brand matters? Let's look at these components more closely in the next chapter to better understand their relevance and importance to your brand.

2

YOUR BRAND
The Key Components That Make It Work

"Your brand had better be delivering something special or it is not going to get the business…"

—*WARREN BUFFETT*

We've already learned that, as a service professional, the strength of your brand determines your value in the marketplace. Strong brands maintain strong mindshare positions. Additionally, I've told you that your brand is made up by its *utility* and how it is *perceived*. Let's take a closer look at what each of these terms mean.

What is Utility?

Utility is the functional use or benefit of a product or service. Every product or service has a specific utility. As an example, while there are many cars on the road that vary by shape, size, and value, they all have a very specific utility in common: they are designed to transport the user from point A to point B. It doesn't matter if you drive a $10,000 car or a $1,000,000 car, they both perform exactly the same utility (comfort and horsepower are another matter!).

For service professionals, **utility** is the very specific work that we have been trained to do and perform for our clients. It is the technical nature of what we do. All of us have many competitors, and each competitor performs in similar ways. For example, bankers offer very similar services within strict guidelines in a highly regulated environment. Accountants handle audits and tax compliance in generally accepted accounting principles. Commercial insurance brokers assess risk and provide coverage against those risks from financially strong insurance companies. Each competitor provides the same utility in dealing with client issues.

The key for all service professionals is to understand that utility encompasses three elements that must be present for the service professional to succeed as a practitioner. Regardless of the craft or skill involved, what matters is:

1. **You know exactly what you do.**

2. **You know why you do it.**

3. **You know precisely who you do it for.**

If you can speak clearly and specifically to these three things, you will create clarity for those who need to understand the utility of what you provide. Clarity is critical to success in today's hyper-competitive environment because your best competition, the competitors who always seem to be around the top prospects that you would love to claim as yours, have a laser-like focus. They always present themselves as the experts and specialists to the very clients you want. Most referral sources seek out specialists who can address the problems and challenges specific to their client's situations. **When a service professional lacks the crystal-clear clarity that telegraphs "specialist" to everyone they encounter, they either won't get any referrals, or will get referrals that waste their time and resources.** By this, I mean "wrong clients"—those who don't meet all of their criteria, aren't best served by their skills, and/ or don't have the need or money for their services.

The way to avoid this problem is to be able to clearly communicate, in layman's terms, what you do so the person you're speaking with can fully grasp the utility you provide. Likewise, you must be able to clearly describe your ideal clients. Think of it as painting a picture of who you best serve. Your goal is to quickly put both a description of what you do and who you do it for neatly into the brain of the person you're speaking with. That way, when someone mentions needing your service, the person will immediately think of you.

And you'll get the call.

Over the years, I have witnessed more lost opportunities simply because people did a lousy job communicating their utility and were not memorable. When you, as a service professional, clearly communicate what you do and the specific markets and market segments you do it for, you separate yourself from the rest of the thundering herd. You stand out in your field! So, people notice, remember you, and think about you—and will likely send you a referral. But, when those who have the potential to send you a referral are unclear about your services and the type of clients you work with, there is very little chance they'll remember you, let alone tell anyone about you.

Over the years, I've met many service professionals who use the flypaper strategy. They found it extremely difficult to limit the types of clients they work with to specific markets and market segments—i.e., to the types of clients who can benefit most from their services. They were afraid doing so would limit their opportunity for business, even though they were eliminating prospects that weren't a good value match for them.

Unfortunately, people who pursue this kind of fly paper strategy usually end up wasting a lot of time and fail to hit their revenue or income goals. Still, some very smart people, the ones with excellent training and top skills, try it because they assume some business is better than no business.

For example, I have worked with a number of financial planners. Though many of them sell and recommend similar products and services, they all tend to specialize in specific markets and market segments. Recently, however, I worked with a very experienced planner who felt he had a better approach. During our first meeting, he told me he was convinced that his best clients could be found in many places. We talked through the issue, and it became clear he was going to have a hard time building his brand around specific types of clients. I came to the conclusion his inability to focus was rooted in one dominant emotion: fear.

Ironically, while this planner feared narrowing his focus would cost him clients and revenue, the exact opposite was true. What he did not realize was that his brand was weak *because* he was not memorable—thereby minimizing the chance of referrals in his sweet spot—the very best client fit for him. As we progress through the chapters, my hope is that you'll see exactly how clarity will work for you and not against you as you gain a fuller understanding of how mindshare works. Knowing clearly who your clients are helps strengthen your brand. The stronger the brand, the greater the chance you will enjoy mindshare in the minds of those who are your best referrers of potential clients.

Many times when I'm starting to work with a new client, I'll ask them what type of clients they like to work with. I know that when they respond with something generic like, "I work with middle-market manufacturers," we have a lot of work to do!

Being able to describe the type of client you work with is a critical component of the utility of your brand. When a referrer of a potential client has a prospect, the first thing that goes through their mind is, "Who do I know who handles this type of client?" **For them to include your name along with others will depend on their recalling what they know about—say it with me—*what you do* and *who you do it for*.** If there is any ambiguity surrounding you and those two ideas, they simply will pass over your name and go on to someone who did a better job articulating their brand.

Given what I just shared with you, would you agree that a service professional who says, "I work with middle-market manufacturers" to describe his ideal clients probably won't come to mind at referral time? There's just not enough meat in that description for it to be memorable.

Okay, role-play time. Let's assume you're an accountant, and one of your clients is a technology manufacturer based in Southern California. You have a long-standing relationship with the owner of this company and he comes to you whenever he needs to make an important decision regarding his company's financial matters. This manufacturer has been a client of yours for five years and you value the relationship both in terms of helping the client, and the revenue it produces for you.

One day, the owner calls you and says he's unhappy with his banker for a myriad of reasons: the guy's hard to get ahold of, doesn't follow up, and, worst of all, acts as though he's doing the owner a favor by banking with him in the first place. The owner, *your* client, asks advice for finding a replacement banker. Specifically, he asks, "Do you know any good replacement candidates? Someone who can help our company get to the next level financially?" You say you'll give it some thought and get back to him with a potential recommendation.

After you get off the phone, you think about who you know who might be a potential solution for your client. Because of the importance of the relationship, you want to make the best choice for the client. Plus, you also want to make sure the person you refer will strengthen your relationship with the client, not detract from it. You think of four individuals you know who are in commercial banking. Because of the size of your client's operations, you immediately dismiss two of the individuals because their banks focus on smaller local operations, while your client's company operates internationally.

Of the two remaining individuals, one is an acquaintance who networks incessantly. You've talked to him at a couple of functions, but don't know him that well. You understand he's in commercial banking with a larger bank and that he works with "middle-market manufacturers." You're not sure what that means, but you do remember that, at least, he works with manufacturers.

The other individual you are considering is also a commercial banker. He works for a good-size bank that could easily handle your client's financial needs. You also met this person at a function, but have gotten to know him a little bit better, because he followed up with you and in fact, reaches out to you on a regular basis with invitations for coffee or lunch. When this individual described the clients he works with, he clearly identified the types who would benefit most from the relationship with him and the bank. One of those descriptions involved manufacturers. You remember his sharing with you that he works with "closely held manufacturing companies based in California that may have multiple operations in various locations, are doing between

$5 million and $50 million a year in revenue, and have a focus in technology or biotechnology products." As it turns out, he painted the perfect picture for you to remember him in this situation.

So I ask you, if you were strictly choosing one of these individuals based upon their utility, who would you pick? In all probability, you immediately dismissed our friend who either wanted to be a generalist or didn't want to take the time to really understand and create the description of his ideal client. **It is important to understand that when any of us make a referral, we are putting our reputations on the line.** Our initial decision-making process centers on utility, because our client is looking for specific skills and capabilities.

It's important to note that you *can* work with more than one market and market segment. In Chapter 7, you will learn how to develop your plan so that you identify specific markets and market segments that will help you achieve your revenue objectives. Just remember, you always want to leave a clear picture of the utility your brand provides in the minds of other professionals you meet.

It is your brand that creates mindshare, and utility is 20% of your brand. The overwhelming reason another professional will refer their client to you and not your competition is their perception of you and what your brand stands for. Perception typically accounts for 80% of the reason your brand is or is not taking up space in the mind of another professional. None of this diminishes the importance of what you do, who you do it for, and why you do it. Your skill, your craft, your knowledge, and your unique abilities are what you bring to the marketplace. If, however, the other professional has a perception of you that is negative in any way, you are probably not going to be in the top position.

Let's take a closer look at why perception is so important in the makeup of your brand.

What is Perception?

Perception is the qualitative impact we have on those we must influence to refer us business. As much as we'd like our work to stand for our brand, the fact is that 80% of what makes our brand is how favorably people perceive us on a personal level.

The perception of your brand must be that you don't merely go through the motions when delivering your service, but that you make things *happen*. **Perception communicates your brand's promise.** You must do more than differentiate yourself from the competition; you must convey that your brand can make a difference. When it comes to winning referrals, your brand's promise trumps the services you provide. Every time.

When a referrer thinks of your name, they will have either a positive or negative impression of your personal brand. The perception someone has of you involves many subjective factors. What they boil down to, however, is: how you present yourself, how you communicate, and whether or not you have what I call "PIP." That is, whether or not you are perceived as being **P**urposeful, **I**ntentional, and **P**assionate about what you do. The banker in the example clearly had the PIP. He took the time to stay connected with you in a purposeful, intentional and passionate manner.

When you meet someone for the first time, you are being quickly assessed. **Most decisions about whether you will be liked or not are made in the first couple of minutes.** As they say, you only get one chance to make a first impression! The way you present yourself to others gives them the information they use to make fast, summary judgments about you. In a flash, they decide things like: Does he have a professional appearance? Is she a good listener? Is he trustworthy? Does she seem sensible, energetic, and full of life? Or does she come across tired, run-down, and burned-out in her job?

Before you meet someone, ask yourself how you want to be remembered. Grooming, clothing, and manners all factor in here. If you come across as sloppy and disinterested, who will want to refer you to a friend or to a valued client? No one, that's who.

You don't have to be the brightest, most up-to-date designer package on the shelf to get noticed, but you *do* need to have an image that is consistent with the brand you want to project and imprint in their minds. For example, if your service is selling guided Safari trips to the Australian Outback, a bowie knife on your belt and a khaki outfit with a slouch hat and hiking boots is appropriate—even if you're taking potential clients to dinner. But, it's a totally different story (and a rather scary one) if you're a CPA specializing in taxes, working with the owners of international businesses.

Many years ago, I was introduced to an estate planning attorney and CPA who came to a ProGrowth event. I could tell he was very intelligent. Unfortunately, he presented himself like the absent-minded professor. He was unkempt and had questionable hygiene. You could guess what he had for breakfast just by what had been spilled on his tie. This man struggled to get clients and I really felt for him. He was the nicest guy you would ever want to meet, but his packaging was so poor that I'm sure it cost him business. Who would want to chance putting him in front of a valued client? He looked disorganized, and the fear that he might also be disorganized in his work made him too much of a risk in the minds of most professionals.

On the other side of the continuum, I got to know a wealth management strategist who worked for himself, but was contracted with a financial services firm. He had the exact opposite problem as the attorney/CPA. Because he was trying to work with higher net worth individuals, he felt that he needed to have a high-dollar image. He wore expensive designer suits, complete with silk pocket squares, alligator shoes, and a gold bracelet around one wrist and expensive watch around the other. He came off as aloof and acted like you should feel honored to be in his presence. In other words, he seemed inauthentic. As a result, he found it difficult to engage other professionals and gain their trust. He reached out to me; I was interested in learning more about the man behind the façade. To my surprise, when I was finally able to get him to "get real," I learned he was a really nice human being who wanted to create a lot of value for others, but was severely hindered by his own insecurities. In many ways, he felt he wasn't good enough at his job to attract the clients he wanted. Therefore, he created a persona in order to be seen as someone who deserves to work with higher net worth people.

We all have blind spots. But, just like products that may be good but are wrapped in bad packaging, we won't get people excited about us if we fail to present ourselves appropriately.

How you communicate—visually and verbally—speaks to your authenticity. I would bet that if I made a lineup of five people, you could probably tell who was being themselves and who was a poseur. Remember when you were first starting in business? You probably were pretty stiff when you met older professionals, because you didn't want to come across as inexperienced, right? Ironically, as you know now, that very unease only called attention to your rookie status!

We all want to do business with people who make us feel comfortable. Since phony people tend to make us feel awkward, they don't make the cut. **As a professional seeking to grow your business, your intentions and concern for others *must* come across as genuine and authentic.** We will look closer at this important concept in Chapter 9, "Authenticity – Being The Real You (And Its Rewards)."

Another factor that affects people's perception is communication style. To gain mindshare, you need to communicate in a way that is interactive and collaborative. Trying to impress a potential referrer with how successful and important you are will only diminish his or her respect for you. In fact, you will be remembered as a pompous and arrogant person who makes everything about you, and who has little or no concern for the potential referrer. **Professionals who are focused on other people's needs are the ones who are remembered—and in a very good way.** As you're about to learn, helping others is a surefire strategy for strengthening your brand, and creating mindshare in the process.

Earlier I shared the concept of "PIP." Are you **P**urposeful, **I**ntentional, and **P**assionate about what you do and who you do it for? Then, you have PIP, an essential ingredient for grabbing mindshare. Someone who is **purposeful** knows where they're going, and more importantly, how they're going to get there. They are steadfast in their resolve and determined to achieve their goals. Being **intentional** is about having a plan, a deliberate and conscious effort that leaves nothing to chance. **Passionate** individuals are known for being spirited, excited, and fervent about creating value for their clients and those that refer business to them.

One thing you need to know about PIP is that it can't be faked. If you are bored with your work and really want to be doing something else, your clients and potential referrers will pick up on it. Don't make the mistake of thinking you can—or should—continue in a profession just because you need an income and don't feel you can do anything else. To be successful at any business requires a lot of hard work and passion for what you do.

If you have the choice of referring someone who has PIP versus someone who is going through the motions and just trying to make their rent payment, I think you'd have your answer in a heartbeat. It should be obvious that having PIP is essential for your brand's success and plays a big role in gaining mindshare!

Perception is the soft side (the intangible quality) of why someone feels stronger about your brand than someone else's. Their perception *is* reality, for all intents and purposes. And, since people value things differently, you will always appeal to some professionals and not to others. But, if we are conscientious about how we present ourselves, communicate, and display our PIP, we can feel confident our brand has a good chance of creating mindshare.

Throughout this book, we will be looking at perceptual issues that can impact your brand. Once these issues are understood and addressed, mindshare then becomes a matter of developing referrer relationships so that you can create a space in the right person's brain that triggers them to call you and not your competition when referral opportunities occur. We'll get into this in more detail in Chapter 4, when we discuss the importance of a relationship (also known as distribution) system.

Before we move onto building these relationships, however, I want to cover some familiar ground in the next chapter. Stay with me, and we'll get to the bottom of why you may be having a difficult time getting the referrals you want. Plus, I'll explain the steps you can take to do something about it.

3

WHY COMPETENT PROFESSIONALS FAIL FINANCIALLY

"We are products of our past, but we don't have to be prisoners of it."

-RICK WARREN

I have had the opportunity and the privilege to know many professionals who were poised for success. They had all the degrees, certificates, and training anyone could ask for. Yet, despite their industry and educational preparation, they struggled to build a referral-generated client base that would drive their business and enable them to attain the success they deserved.

There are a number of reasons this happens, but I have determined they boil down to ten major issues, any one of which can prevent mindshare from occurring. In each of the following chapters, we will learn how to identify and address these issues. For now, let's take a brief look at what happens when one or more of these issues is present, and how they negatively impact your ability to gain mindshare.

Issue #1: Not Understanding How To Connect With A Person's Social Style

Personal connection is the very first step to creating mindshare.

None of us is going to refer someone we don't feel good about personally. And, you are more willing to get to know someone—you're actually *drawn* to them, in fact—when you sense compatibility. It's a feeling of familiarity that naturally puts you at ease, and makes you comfortable with who the person is.

Sadly, I have seen many professionals fail at attempts to engage with someone simply because they didn't know how to modify their behavior so that they could connect with the other person. This is a common problem; even expert communicators cannot successfully peg every person's social style.

Those who never consider the power social styles play in their relationships are oblivious to the ramifications it is having on their business. They sweep right by it because they're only interested in what they can *get* from people, not in how they can *help* them.

Have you ever sat down with someone who immediately starts trying to sell you something or begins talking all about themselves? If you're a professional who is gracious with your time and respectful of others, you probably sat there nodding your head and feigning interest, even though the whole time you were thinking, "Man, I cannot *wait* until this meeting is over."

Because you were attentive and the other person is completely self-centered, he or she likely believed you were mightily impressed by him or her. At the conclusion of the meeting, you shake the person's hand and walk away thinking, "Yikes! Glad that's done. Never again!" Meanwhile, the other person leaves thinking, "Touchdown!" convinced you will be sending scores of referrals his or her way. What a disconnect—and, unfortunately, a fairly common occurrence. Clearly, you'll have no desire to pursue an ongoing relationship with this individual. The potential for any type of relationship or mindshare from you died an early death simply because that person didn't take time to appreciate you and your social style, and how to interact favorably with you. Had they been still and engaging, and listened to you, and made the effort to speak your language, things could have gone much differently.

Understanding how you relate to others will allow you to properly assess another person's social style. When you relate to others in a way that respects that style, you will connect faster, better, and stronger. Again, connecting is an essential first step in creating the mindshare you want. In fact, it is so integral to creating mindshare that we have devoted Chapter 6 "Your Are A Rainmaker – It's Just A Matter Of Understanding" entirely to the art of connecting. The skill begins with knowing your own social style so you can have more confidence and self-assurance in the way you relate to others.

I believe everyone possesses the ability to be a rainmaker. An important quality is to comprehend and embrace our social style, and authentically modify our behavior in a way that leverages it.

Issue #2: Lacking Clarity In The Utility Of Your Business

A lack of clarity about who they serve best has been the bane of many technically sharp professionals. When you cannot articulate the clear and precise utility of your brand, you are cooking up a recipe for a suffering business. Unfortunately, this inability is all too commonplace among competent service professionals.

People assume that if they are a banker, commercial real estate broker, accountant, attorney, or some other profession that others readily grasp what they do and who they do it for.

Nothing could be further from the truth.

I have seen many experienced professionals have the chance to make their mark in a group setting, only to fumble badly when they had the spotlight—and the floor. Have you ever wanted to meet with someone who you thought might be a great referral source, only to walk away from a conversation with him or her totally clueless about what he or she actually does—and for whom? **If you cannot clearly and concisely explain to others what SERVICE you provide and who you best serve, you cannot expect people to send CLIENTS your way.** You have handicapped your potential network of people—and handed your competition the ball.

Worse, your lack of clarity sends a message that you either do not take your business seriously or that you take the fly paper approach to business development—i.e., you make a grab at anyone and everyone who comes along. In other words, you appear unfocused and directionless. Everyone wants to work with people who know where they're going and how they're going to get there. If your actions suggest that you're a catch-it-all type of person, expect people to point their referrals elsewhere.

In Chapter 7, we will help you avoid these types of situations by showing you how to create a vision and a clear plan for your business. Not only will this boost your confidence, but it will let people know you are purposeful and on top of your game. You *will* know exactly where you are going and how you are going to get there. Our map won't let you down!

Issue #3: Communicating A Poor Value Proposition

One of the main considerations in choosing a potential referral partner is the perceived value he or she offers to the clients referred to them. We call this a **"value proposition."** The authors of *Rainmaking Conversations*, Mike Shultz and John Doerr, point out that a good value proposition statement is a collection of reasons why someone will want to work with you. These reasons satisfy the following needs:

1. Prospects want and need what you're offering. You have to <u>resonate</u> with them.

2. Prospects need to be able to see how you stand out from your competition and that you are the best option. You have to <u>differentiate</u> yourself.

3. Prospects need to believe that you can <u>deliver</u> on your promises. You must be able to substantiate your ability to perform.

These elements create a three-legged stool. If you remove one leg (i.e., satisfaction of a need), the stool will collapse. Likewise, if you fail to convey a well-thought-out value proposition, it will affect your ability to influence another professional much less the prospect themself.

I think you would agree, there is a big difference between articulating the *value* that you bring versus the *technical aspects* of what you do. Anyone can get a "technician," but getting someone who understands your needs and desires as a client and what needs to be done to meet those needs and desires is very different. There are many technicians out there who struggle because they don't view clients as unique human beings whose lives have ups and downs. To them, a client is just another case, just another application of their trade. None of us want that type of person serving us (as a client), or representing us (as a referrer). But, those who can articulate their value get the attention of others and do a great job setting themselves apart from the rest of the thundering herd. And people want to refer clients to these articulate "herd defectors," because doing so reflects well on them—which indirectly strengthens their own brand. It's what you call a win-win situation.

Issue #4: You Are Not Being Authentic

Shakespeare said, "To thine own self be true" several hundred years ago. That saying is still true today. People want to do business with people who are real. Those who appear to stand for nothing, or trying to be someone they're not, or seem to have no belief system or values stand little chance of gaining mindshare.

Most people are turned off by phonies. When somebody is not comfortable with who they are and feel they need to create a persona to win business, they fool no one and their efforts will backfire. The problem is most people trying to be someone other than themselves are not aware of how they come across! They are posers trying to get referrals, and most people can see right through them.

Let's take that a step further. Imagine you and I are sitting with a friend who is an attorney. The three of us have been meeting for the past year to exchange ideas and potential prospects, and to make introductions for people who may be helpful to one another. Our friend, "George," has attended these meetings for the last six month, and keeps lamenting how difficult it is for him to continue practicing law. He wishes there were something else he could do to make a living, but with a mortgage and a family to support, he feels stuck. While you and I really empathize with poor George, we're also finding it more and more difficult to try to help him. It's clear that he's not passionate about what he does, and that his level of interest is to only do the minimum needed to solve a client issue and get paid for the work he performed.

Privately, you and I have agreed that we're not comfortable putting George in front of a prospect. Nor are we comfortable introducing him to other professionals, because they'll see what we see: a guy who doesn't enjoy helping people through his profession. They would question why we even made the introduction. It puts you and me in a very difficult position, because we're dealing with someone who, while experienced at what he does, is not authentic about his work. He merely does it because it's the path of least resistance and pays his bills. As you may have guessed, George is not very successful. His business suffers because he is stuck in a negative cycle and simply is not getting the number of referrals he wants—for a job he no longer enjoys doing. As painful as it is, you and I ultimately decide we can't help George, and inform him we are disbanding the group.

Besides being true to ourselves, authenticity also requires us to genuinely want to create value for others. Because George lacked passion for his profession, he had no motivation to use it to help his clients—the few clients he had. Sadly, he viewed his job as a means to an end: a paycheck. I guarantee you this attitude affected his ability to grow his law practice. Being authentic is critical to creating mindshare. In Chapter 9, "Authenticity – Being The Real You (And Its Rewards)," we'll look closely at the other key components of authenticity. As we do, you'll understand more and more why authenticity is so important.

Issue #5: You Are Too Focused On Just Networking

In a hyper-competitive environment, it's easy to get caught up in the vortex of networking, especially if you justify your activity by telling yourself that more is better. The fact is that networking—at least the way most people do it—yields no new business.

Because the time and energy involved are not being properly directed, networking often ends up being completely ineffective.

In a contracting economy, such as we experienced after the crash in 2007, service professionals find themselves in a completely different macro-economic environment. Where it was once easy to find clients, the new reality is that there are now more service professionals in all disciplines than at any time in history, and a shrinking pie made up of fewer clients. This is in stark contrast to previous years of prosperity, where it seemed good clients could be found everywhere. This game changer made one thing clear: to be of value to their firm, service professionals must not only do quality work, but drive revenue by bringing in new clients.

It is during these times of disruptions that service professionals suddenly become aware of other networking tools such as LinkedIn, Facebook, and Twitter. They hear it's the new way to get prospects, and they'll look out of touch if they don't jump online and "start getting their name out there." So, they sign up, build profiles, join networking groups, start attending functions, and pass out lots and lots of business cards, in the hopes they will get referrals they need to meet their sales objectives. They see all this networking busyness as chances to feather their nests, instead of what it really should be: opportunities to learn they can help others.

They're only being human.

Because of what I do, I touch a lot of people. From time to time, individuals contact me under the guise that they want to learn more about our program. I am happy to meet with anyone who wants to improve his or her business and life. Once, I met with such a person, at his request, at a social club I belong to in Newport Beach. I saw it as an opportunity to learn more about him and what he'd like to accomplish, and agreed to meet him for coffee in one of the club's restaurants.

This man, who we'll call "Peter," began by telling me he did financial planning with a primary focus on selling life insurance. First thing I noticed was that, for the type of business he was in, Peter didn't present himself very well. He was somewhat disheveled and clearly unshaven. This immediately sent up red flags up for me. Within five minutes, it was obvious that Peter's strategy was all about playing a numbers game. I detected he had zero interest in me or my program. What Peter *was* interested in were all the people I had access to at the club. Throughout our conversation, his eyes kept darting around the room, hoping to find someone else he could network with. Eventually, I leaned back in my chair and stopped talking.

Peter is what I consider a classic example of "the incessant networker." He's the type of person who plays the networking numbers game, hoping to pull someone into his vortex of busyness and disconnection, and to grab a referral or two along the way. I'm willing to bet he has four to five meetings with new individuals each week, and probably attends two or three networking events.

While I found myself angry that I wasted my time meeting with Peter, I also felt empathy for him, because I understand how challenging his business can be in this environment. He was trying to provide for his family. Unfortunately, he was doing so using a very difficult strategy that will keep him from enjoying the life he wants.

Because of this pressure to produce new business, it's easy to get caught up in thinking that investing time and energy in networking groups will somehow make a difference. Attending a myriad of functions and pressing the flesh deludes one into believing that business will start rolling in. Yet, since there's no direction to all these efforts, your ability to get results is hindered.

Because of the post-2007 change in our economy and recessions that will surely come in the future, it is vital you understand clearly where your opportunities lie.

None of this is meant to disparage the importance of networking. Obviously, a service provider cannot build a business alone. In fact, networking is more important than ever in today's hyper-competitive environment. But, to be worth your time and energy, it must be the right kind of networking, with a pre-determined purpose that accomplishes stated goals. It should only take place to facilitate a process—a process that will identify specific individuals with whom you build a relationship system that will produce predictable results and create a mutual ability to help one another.

In Chapter 4, "A Distribution System is a Must", we'll take a close look at what you can do to avoid the pitfalls of depending on the randomness of networking.

Issue#6: You Cannot Differentiate Yourself

If you cannot give people a reason to choose you over your competition . . . why should they? In a highly-competitive environment, you'll just come across as another "me too." Likewise, it's critical that you build your brand in the mind of someone who's in a position to send their clients to you. Your brand, which is your name and everything it stands for, must be distinctive in the mind of the referrer. Remember, everything you do—from meetings to functions to having lunch—is a marketing event that affects your individual brand. Those who don't take marketing events seriously and are not actively working on their business end up having weak brands.

Being another "me too" in an economy that's on fire probably isn't as tough a situation as being in a hyper-competitive environment where people have many choices. **It's critical to your success to build a strong presence in specific markets and market segments.** As I will keep repeating in this book, **it is not in your best interests to try to be all things to all people.** On the contrary, this unfocused approach will weaken your brand and make it difficult for you to gain any mindshare with potential referrers.

It is important to realize that you can't rely solely on the utility of what you do to carry your brand. Bright professionals who have amazing technical skills often make the mistake of assuming their work will drive their success. They believe that they can differentiate themselves solely on the basis of being a great technician or a gifted professional. Unfortunately, that's not true. A famous quote by John C. Maxwell says it all:

"People do not care how much you know until they know how much you care."

Doing great work gets you to the starting line along with everybody else who does great work. So, the question is, "How do you become that go-to person someone thinks of whenever they have a high-quality referral?" Since 80% of your brand is based upon perception, the answer is, "By clearly differentiating yourself in a number of ways." That's how you create the all-important space in someone's mind that we call mindshare.

Chapters 6, 7, 8, 9, 10 and 11 all cover a number of issues that will help your referral sources perceive you favorably.

Issue #7: Your Focus Is On Quantity And Not Quality

Some professionals measure their success by the number of names they have in their contact management system and not by the depth of their relationships with others. They are more comfortable meeting a large number of people at various networking events and religiously adding names to their large database of individuals than truly "connecting" with a single person.

Focusing on quantity rather than quality will always impede one's ability to create mindshare. If somehow this type of person is ever able to achieve some level of mindshare, it will quickly wane, since there will unlikely be any follow-up or attempt to get to know individuals on a more intimate level. For these professionals, taking the time to sit and really get to know someone is actually considered a liability. They will typically see engagement and interaction as too time-consuming. Why spend that much time with one person, when they can hit a networking event and troll around for lots of business cards?

We've all come across this type of individual. I think you would agree with me that, for the most part, whether they're aware of it or not, these people struggle to gain the respect of others. The mistake they make is not getting to know the professionals who can refer business to them. As a result, if and when referrals come, they are typically weak and off point.

Chapter 5, "The ProGrowth Relationship System (PRS) – Making Your Competition Irrelevant," will convince you there is a better approach than the "numbers game" that will make you more effective and efficient in developing the right relationships.

Issue #8: You Are Depending On Acquaintances To Come Through For You

Professionals who are focused on meeting and collecting as many business cards as they can depend on acquaintances rather than relationships to help them grow their business. Relying on acquaintances for referrals actually heightens the competitiveness—with the outcome being a far less likely chance of getting meaningful referrals. It's not that the acquaintances are bad people; they're simply busy, just like you are. While you may believe you've made a strong enough impression to keep them thinking about you, unfortunately, you're wrong. Your brand is not strong enough in their minds for them to think of you when the need for your services arises—particularly if they have four or five other acquaintances who do exactly what you do. In fact, if these people you barely know haven't seen you in a while, you can bet one of the other acquaintance they've made—whoever is most recent—has stronger mindshare than you do. You have become yesterday's news!

Some individuals like this casual approach much better than building deeper relationships. They don't like to do a lot of follow-up or take the time to really get to know someone. They feel time and energy spent getting to know someone better will only cost them the chance to meet more people. It's like skimming the surface of the ocean, rather than diving beneath. While you will cover more area swimming on top of the water, taking the time to explore its depths would actually afford you a more memorable experience.

The same is true with people.

Developing a relationship system is the only way that you can really make your competition irrelevant. Again, in Chapter 5, we'll take a close look at this very important topic, and offer you solutions on how to create deeper relationships that make you, and not your competition, memorable.

Issue #9: Instead Of A Plan, You Use Hope As A Strategy

One of the major reasons some people are disappointed with their end-of-year results is that they had no plan in place to get what they wanted. Many of the people I come across begin each year by simply telling themselves that they need to get out and repeat what they did last year to see if they can get some referrals. That's not a plan. It's using hope as a strategy. If these people were disappointed with last year's results; what makes them think this year's will be any different?

One of the key benefits of having a plan is that it gives you a blueprint for the results you want to achieve. It's like building a house. Before you build a house, you have an architect draw up a set of plans that your contractor will use to ensure the results you want. The contractor follows the plan so that he can build the house you envisioned. There may be issues that come up, but having strategies and tactics in place to address them keep you on track to getting the house you wanted.

For you to build the business that you want, you likewise need a plan—a "business blueprint"—to achieve the business and income you want. By following your plan, you will not waste time doing things that won't get you where you want to be. In Chapter 7, "Professional Goals – Know Your Target And How You'll Hit It," you'll learn how a plan will invigorate you and give you a sense of purpose in reaching your goals. You will also learn why a plan is vitally important to creating mindshare to get the referrals you want.

Issue# 10: Your Business Has No Distribution System It Can Count On

Every good business depends on a distribution system to get its products or services into the hands of those who will benefit from them. Look around you. Everything you see and use has been brought to you by the company that manufactured it through a distribution channel that was committed to getting that product into your hands. For example, I'm writing this book on my Mac. While I think the Mac is a great product, it wouldn't be sitting on my desk if Apple had no reliable way of distributing it. A well-thought-out distribution system is critical to the success of a business. It's no different for service businesses. One of the primary reasons many professionals struggle is that they don't have a clear-cut distribution system—or, in our vernacular, *a relationship system*, to capture the clients they want. Instead, they're totally dependent on random referrals that may or may not ever come. And, if hope and randomness do happen to bring a referral your way, there's a high likelihood that referral won't be of the quality you would like.

In Chapter four, you will learn the importance of having a well thought out relationship system, and the critical role it plays in gaining the mindshare that will enable you to build a more predictable business.

My intent in writing this chapter was not to be negative, but to give you a better sense of the issues that can impede your ability to gain mindshare and achieve your goals. In reading it, you may even have identified one or more issues that are holding you back! I hope you agree after reading this chapter that **mindshare does not just happen**. Rather, it takes a conscientious effort and an understanding of what mindshare requires in order to get it. Starting with the next chapter, we are going to look at specific things you can do to gain mindshare with people who can help you grow your business.

4

A DISTRIBUTION SYSTEM IS A MUST

"Success is almost totally dependent upon drive and persistence. The extra energy required to make another effort or try another approach is the secret of winning."

—*DENIS WAITLEY*

In many ways, we service professionals are not much different than the companies that manufacture the products we use every day. These companies spend millions and millions of dollars to create new products that satisfy the needs of their current and future customers. As good as the products may be, they only have *value* when they get into the hands of those customers. Therefore, companies must ensure customers can easily and conveniently obtain their products.

As marketing authority Phillip Kotler has noted, marketing distribution channels are critical to the success of any business. From a classical marketing sense, distribution decisions are extremely important because they determine how a company's customers access and purchase their products. While companies understand the importance of having a dependable product distribution system, they also understand that this system can be expensive and time-consuming. The key is that the system must be worth the effort. The company must be able to continually educate its channel partners on its products. The company must also work closely with its partners and show them how the relationship will create value and can be mutually profitable. From the company's perspective, the effort is well worth it. In order for a company to achieve its objectives, its distribution system must be both effective and efficient. This can only happen with channel partners who have a deep relationship with the company and know and understand its products. Smart companies know that if they don't continually nurture those relationships, they will wither—and competitors will jump at the chance to take their place.

If you think about it, don't we have similar issues? Since you're reading this book, I'm confident you have great technical skills and want to expose those skills to the clients who can benefit from using your services. Do you have a distribution system that you can absolutely count on? If you are like most service professionals, your distribution system is weak at best, because you probably depend on the randomness of networking.

Kotler defines a distribution channel as a set of interdependent organizations (intermediaries) involved in the process of making a product or service available for use or consumption. **He asserts that channel decisions will directly affect every other marketing decision.**

Marketing channels are typically used because the cost and/or amount of time required don't warrant a direct marketing channel. Direct marketing means that a business does all of its own lead generation and sales development directly, such as through cold calling. As a service provider, you *are* the product, so it doesn't make sense to use direct marketing to attract clients. Why? Because what you provide is relevant to potential clients *only* when a specific need arises. **To be continually contacting those who**

may never have a need for your services or infrequently have a need is not a good use of your time.

If you provide services, you've probably depended on a three-channel distribution system to market them. The channels include:

1. Other service professionals who potentially have access to clients in need of your services.

2. Clients who have experienced your services and are willing to share their satisfaction with potential clients.

3. "Friends of the firm" who know you and are willing to share your name and expertise if the opportunity presents itself.

Networking – Is It Really The Answer?

Networking with other service professionals is likely where you spend most of your marketing time. You anticipate that the hours and chitchat invested will eventually produce the clients you want. So, you join one or two networking groups and attend an array of networking events passing out cards and pressing the flesh. You cross your fingers and hope the people you meet will think of you if an opportunity presents itself to refer your services.

So, is what you're doing effective? Is it getting you results? Having *any* impact on your business? One of the most critical components of networking concerns the commitment these other professionals have to you—or not. Face it: Most people you meet are *acquaintances*. They are not people with whom you have *relationships*.

Big difference.

Acquaintances aren't set up with a clearly defined purpose and intention. If these people aren't committed to your product or service, but are willing to act if (by chance) the right situation is presented, guess what? In all likelihood, they'll actually miss those opportunities to refer you. Why? Simple. Your brand is very weak in their minds and, in all probability, you are way down the list of the people they might consider—if they remember you at all. They are far more likely to give "your" referral to a competitor of yours—some professional they met more recently.

If you recall from our earlier discussion, unless you are in the referrer's number one or number two mindshare position, chances are slim that you will get the call. When you attend networking functions and meetings, everyone is "on the hunt"—just like you are—for that one opening, that prized carrot, when someone *somehow* offers a good referral. Sure, you have to "give to get," but that doesn't kill the hope that someone will give you that quality referral. It's human nature to look at things from a "what's in it for me" perspective; rarely if at all do people network with a plan to give referrals to some other networker in return.

In an environment where macroeconomic issues affect you negatively (through no fault of your own), don't be delusional and treat that new reality—the crowded and potentially anonymizing world of networking—as "business as usual." You could invest a lot of time networking and hope for the best, but receive nothing in return.

Similarly, networking websites such as LinkedIn show dramatic increases in unique visitors and extended site visits in a hyper-competitive environment. Facebook and Twitter also experience significant increases in membership and activity from those using it for business networking purposes. **Successful**

marketing through online networks also requires intention and purpose.

People who enjoyed the benefits of the strong economy had a run of almost 10 years (1997-2007). But reality hits hard when things turn around. Some service professionals have since seen their revenue and their stable of regular clients shrink to dangerously low levels, just because the pie is smaller and there are more professionals than ever competing for pieces. They realize that their value is based on the quality of work they do for their clients and the revenue they drive to their firms, yet they may not have the volume of business they're used to. So, networking becomes a defensive measure.

Webster's dictionary defines networking as "the developing of contacts or exchanging of information with others in an informal network, as to further a career." That definition implies the beginning of a process aimed at getting a result, yet the way that "development" is pursued is completely random; although you are far from people's busy minds, you are depending merely on the fact that you are a "contact" that these very people will think of you at the appropriate time and send you a business referral. If you are in a highly competitive market, can you afford to leave your distribution channels to chance like this?

In the alternative, what if you had a relationship system that could produce the results you want with a high degree of probability? Yes, it would still involve getting referrals from other service providers, **but when you add intention and purpose to the mix, each person in your relationship system becomes a dependable distributor of your services.**

Like anything worthwhile, setting up a viable distribution channel requires the right effort, which, in turn, requires building and managing a process. **But it is a marathon, not a sprint.**

Your relationship system is an asset that will produce results for you for many years to come and create more value for you in the marketplace. And, no one can ever take it away from you.

You'll catapult your business and life to a whole new level.

In Chapter 7, "Professional Goals – Know Your Target And How You'll Hit It," we'll be developing your vision and plan to get the results you want. Once you have determined the market and market segments your clients will come from, you'll have a clear understanding of the types of professionals you need to create a distribution system that can deliver the clients you want. In essence, you want distributors (relationships) who are committed to bringing you clients. I'll walk you through how to get them.

Our distribution system is our relationship system. **The Pro-Growth Relationship System is a distribution system which focuses on a limited number of relationships (your distributors) that can deliver the clients you want while making your competition irrelevant.** Instead of going a mile wide and an inch deep, we like to say we go an inch wide a mile deep. Translation? It is about quality, not quantity. Just remember that you become a distributor for your distributor as well, and, with that, you have a responsibility to their success. Mutual responsibility equals mutual success. Isn't that what we all want? My experience confirms that you can absolutely have it.

Here's the catch. A distribution system is not something that happens overnight. It takes time to build and more time to ensure that it will produce the results you want. **But, if you do it the right way, it will produce *predictable* results for you for many years to come.**

Some people like networking because it does not require any work. It's acceptable—and the norm—to simply show up at meetings, functions, and events. But as we have discussed, and you probably know, a networking prescription will give you a temporary cure (i.e., an up-and-down business) at best. Stick with me, because I'm about to let you in on some secrets that will help you build a great relationship system that can have a real and steady impact on your business. It's time to introduce you to the ProGrowth Relationship System!

5

THE PROGROWTH RELATIONSHIP SYSTEM
Making Your Competition Irrelevant

"You don't sell to distributors.
You sell through them and with them."
—*PHILIP KOTLER*

The ProGrowth Relationship System (PRS), developed more than eighteen years ago, has helped hundreds of professionals build businesses that get predictable results.

For starters, the PRS is about helping **you** be very effective in attracting the clients **you** want, while simultaneously helping you be very efficient in the time that you allocate for your business development. Let me emphasize: This is a *system*. **A system is a number of steps or parts designed to create a specific result. Every step of each part must be done with commitment and without trying to take shortcuts.**

PRS is a systematic distribution channel of service professionals who serve as each other's distributors. You have qualified each individual to become a distributor for your business by conducting a thorough due diligence process. The common objective is to help you and your distributor develop one significant event over the course of the year. This event consists of a direct client involvement or, in the alternative, an introduction and relationship with another referral source that could result in multiple referrals. Either of those events have the potential to be significant for you and/or your distributor.

How PRS Works

As in any system, PRS is a process with a predetermined objective. **Here, it's to create a Level I relationship with each of your distributors, where:**

1. **You both will be in the number one mindshare position for your particular service.**

2. **There is a commitment to each other to get the result you both want.**

Pay particular attention to this process, as it is one of the critical secrets in creating mindshare. In fact, you may want to consider rereading this section a couple of times until you are conversant with it.

As the graphic below illustrates, you should think of PRS as consisting of three "buckets." Individuals enter your relationship system through the Level II door or **"incubator,"** bucket. As you go through your Level II due diligence, the individual will keep "moving up," or they will be removed from the relationship system. "Moving up" means making it through the vetting process and advancing to the Level I **"predictability"** bucket or the Level 3 "assurance" bucket. Clearly, the goal is to be able to take someone and develop them into a Level I relationship. On a rare occasion, you will have a Level 3 relationship. This bucket signifies a relationship similar to Level I, in that the personal relationship is strong, but differs in that the market segments are not very well aligned. You will learn more about Level 3 in the pages just ahead.

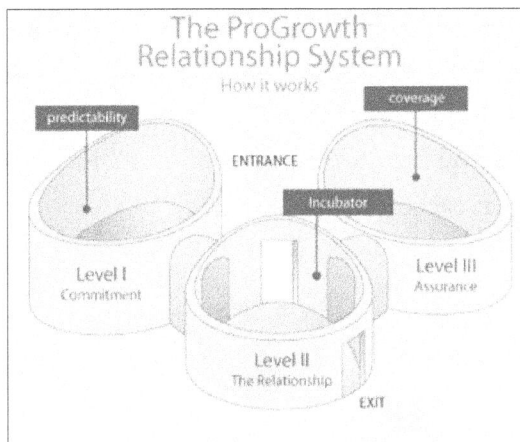

The Level II bucket is called the "incubator" because, just as in a laboratory, you need to make a thorough assessment to determine if the results you want can occur and reoccur—no shortcuts allowed. You are looking for some very special relationships that meet very specific criteria. Individuals who don't meet the tests to "move up" to a Level I or a Level 3 relationship must exit the PRS. In other words, they return to your contact management system (CMS) and remain as a "friend of the firm."

Individuals advance to the Level I bucket when they have met all the tests and cleared the hurdles as a Level II candidate. The commitment that's in place, and that results from an explicit agreement, will predictably deliver one significant event each year.

On a rare occasion, you may have known an individual for many years and have a great personal relationship with him or her, but your two market segments just don't match up well despite your being in similar markets. In this case, you may want to move the person to the Level 3 bucket. For those in this bucket, you agree to keep your antennas up for each other. It's possible you may be able to help one another with something over the course of the year. In essence, you're providing **"coverage"** for each other. However, the goal of PRS is to create Level I relationships and not focus on Level 3 relationships. Think of Level 3 as a rare exception in your PRS.

Now that you have an overview of how PRS works, let's take a closer look at each of the buckets.

Level II – The Relationship Bucket

The Level II vetting process is critically important to developing the Level I relationship. It is a specific process and cannot be rushed. I liken the process to a ripening tomato. Tomatoes start out green. As they begin to ripen, they turn golden. When they're ready to pick, they are a vibrant red. The ripening tomato process cannot be rushed. It must run its course. As you will see, taking someone through the Level II process will be very similar. We like to say that when someone comes into the PRS, the relationship we have with them is like a green tomato: immature, uncertain, and possibly full of juicy promise!

You must be patient and nurture your relationships. They must clear three hurdles if they are to advance to Level I in your PRS. The first hurdle, where the relationship is "green," is known as Level IIC. If the relationship makes it past this hurdle, the second hurdle is Level IIB, known as "golden." If the relationship gets over that hurdle and is still in the running, the third hurdle is Level IIA, which is "red." If the relationship makes it through the three-hurdle process, you will then be able to convert it into that coveted Level I relationship. As with dating, the old axiom is true: You must kiss a lot of "frogs" to find the "prince!" Only, in this case, the prince is a red tomato. Just to give you a heads up on the odds here, developing Level I relationships typically requires eight to ten Level II candidates—most of whom will *not* clear the three hurdles. This is where traditional networking may come in handy. Networking events are places to meet Level II candidates. They are not important...unless they prove over time, to ripen in your PRS.

All of the people you will put into your relationship system will be good people. But remember: You are looking for some very special relationships that will be meaningful over time. The moment you know a relationship can't clear one of the hurdles, remove it from the PRS, so you can focus on the ones who might. Those you remove from the system aren't bad individuals: they're simply meant to remain a "friend of the firm," who will be in your contact management system (CMS). One of my coaching clients put it this way: **"In PRS, people are either moving up to Level I, situated at Level I, or out of your relationship system altogether."** This is a very important concept to grasp to manage your system properly.

Let's examine the characteristics of each hurdle and see why all three are important in making the right decision for the Level I relationship.

Level IIC – Can You Establish Rapport?

When you make the decision that you are interested in someone becoming a Level I relationship and put him or her in your PRS, the first step or hurdle is Level IIC. At this point, think of the person as the proverbial "green tomato." **Level IIC is characterized by the likability factor**. That is, you need to determine if you feel chemistry with the individual. Are you able to establish rapport? In your gut, do you feel like you can build long-term trust with this person?

In all probability, you won't refer service professionals you know unless you feel comfortable with them on a personal level. Not surprisingly, a big mistake that prevents people from taking relationships to Level I is not getting to know individuals well enough. **They fail to recognize that it is the *personal* relationship that provides the foundation of the *business* relationship.** Some professionals blow right by this critical step, because they are so focused on what they can *get* from the individual as opposed to *getting to know* the individual.

Why is this important? I think you would agree that none of us is ever going to refer anyone unless we feel good about him or her as a person first. **Being able to work with an individual you respect, trust, enjoy spending time with, *like*—and who makes you feel totally comfortable with—is very important when you consider who you would *want* to put in front of one of your clients.** You're looking to establish a very special relationship that has the potential of being very productive for both of you over a number of years. Making sure that you enjoy being with that individual is important because, if you don't, the relationship will fail in spite of any business opportunities.

So what are you looking for? My experience suggests that you are looking for specific traits that will give you the comfort to move potential relationships forward. Consider these ten characteristics as you get to know people:

1. **They take an interest in you.** The conversation is not all about them. Even though you ask them questions, you

want them to find ways to learn more about you to lay the groundwork for a good partnership.

2. **They don't have a need to do all the talking and dominate the conversation.** This tells you they're open to hearing you and probably won't make the relationship all about them.

3. **They show qualities of kindness and compassion.** In your conversations with them, it's important that they speak highly of others and show compassion for friends and loved ones. A definite red flag: those who come across as uncaring and say bad things about other people in their conversation. You know that cliché about being able to spot unkind people by how rude they are to restaurant servers? Avoid that type. You want to partner with professionals who have a natural respect for all people.

4. **They're energetic and display a zest for life.** This reveals that they feel good about who they are and shows that their personal lives are on solid ground.

5. **They're ambitious and approach their work and their lives with excitement.** You want to align with people who are optimistic and like to learn, explore, and gain from new experiences—just like you do.

6. **They are open to new ideas and progress.** You want to align with people who are willing to look at fresh perspectives that may make you both more efficient and effective.

7. **They demonstrate humility.** Communicating in a humble way tells you they're comfortable in their own skin

and don't have a need to embellish their position or credentials.

8. **They are honest.** Listen to see if they willingly tell the facts, don't "lie by omission," and take responsibility for their actions. They should also demonstrate an ability to see situations for what they are.

9. **They are even-keeled by nature, not always riding an emotional roller coaster.** You want to work with people who can keep a cool head and will see things through. You *don't* want to partner with people who are moody and bring drama—so that you're always wondering who's going to "show up" on a given day.

10. **They are reliable in all areas of their lives.** It's extremely important to work with others who take their commitments seriously and will be there when you need them. We all have occasional issues that throw us a curve, but regular flakiness has no place in your PRS.

If you're comfortable with individuals who possess these characteristics, you're probably considering the right people for your PRS. Need a way to quantify the process? For every candidate, score each characteristic on a scale of 1 to 10, as follows:

Score of 7 - 10 = Satisfactory to outstanding
Score of 4 - 6 = Poor to unsatisfactory
Less than 4 = Unacceptable

Total up the points for all answers. If someone's score totals 70 or more, you likely have a good candidate to consider.

Someone who scores between 60 and 70 is "borderline," so

you'll want to look at all characteristics again even more closely. If that person scores low in a characteristic you believe is vital to the relationship, you may decide to pass. Always check your "gut." What is it saying to you about this person? You don't want to get down the road only to find that the one or two characteristics that sent up little red flags early on should have precluded the relationship from moving forward.

If the person's total for the 10 characteristics is under 60, remove him or her from your relationship system. That might be difficult if you think the individual can get you in front of potential clients. But, I assure you, you'll be much better off without that person in the long run. **Remember, your relationship system must be comprised of only a few extremely special relationships that work for you.** "Hoping" someone will come through won't provide a strong foundation for your PRS. You will invest meaningful time in this process, so you want to make sure it is time well spent with the right individuals.

How long do you keep someone at this vetting stage? That depends on how well you rate them on the ten characteristics above, and what your gut is telling you. If after your first meeting you don't have a clear sense what you should do, get together with the person again soon. Multiple meetings are good because they provide a chance to see different facets of someone's personality. Plus, just like with dating, people are usually on their best behavior in a first meeting. It is only during a second or third meeting that you begin to get a good sense of who they really are.

This first hurdle of establishing rapport is a very important step in developing the mindshare you want. For both of you to feel good about the relationship, you have to feel good about each other personally. By the way, that "feeling" is all about your perception of the other person. Remember good old perception? As we learned in Chapter 2, "Your Brand – The Key Components That Make It Work," perception makes up 80% of your brand, so it will be a key element in gaining the mindshare you want. It is the same for the person you are considering for your PRS. If you are feeling good about the person at this stage, it's time to move them to Level IIB.

Level IIB – Can You Help Each Other?

Once the relationship has passed Level IIC, the "tomato" is considered golden: it is not yet ripe, but it looks to be heading that direction. **Once you've selected people you can work with on a personal level, you must now determine whether you have the ability to help them.** Yes, find out if *you* can help *them*, not if they can help you. Is there a potential mutual benefit from forming an alliance? Put another way, are you playing in the same sandbox?

Level IIB requires determining whether those you're considering for Level I relationships have clients in the same market and market segments as you. Be patient as you do a thorough job of understanding their practices and the type of clients they work with. You could rush to judgment, invest a lot of time and energy, and learn that your businesses target different clients in either different markets or different market segments. You won't be able to help each other and you've lost valuable time. **You can continue to have an outstanding personal relationship and commit to each other's success, but if you're not playing in the same sandbox, it's not a fit.**

As you will learn in Chapter 7, "Professional Goals – Know Your Target And How You'll Hit It," you have to get specific about your markets and market segments. **Unfortunately, most people**

you will deal with (unless they have read this book!) don't clearly articulate these. That's why it's helpful to have one or two meetings to thoroughly understand each other's business—and ensure that both your markets and market segments are a good match.

For example, if one of the common markets for you and your candidate were manufacturing companies and you both use the term "middle market" (roughly, small to medium-sized companies) to describe your target company, it might seem you both work with similar companies. However, some people use the term "middle market" to describe companies that do $5 to $25 million in revenue, others think it means $25 million to $75 million, and still others think it means $75 million to $200 million in revenue. Now, there's a huge difference between a $5 million level and a $200 million level in terms of what a company might need in terms of services.

Reading this book should help you get super clear about your own markets and market segments. Interestingly enough, you might have to "coach" your candidates through the same identification process you went through. Take your time. Let Level IIB candidates know you want to make sure you can help them. You'll need to peel back the layers of the onion to gain the clarity you want about their business to make sure you are making the right decision. Again, it could take two to three interactions with a candidate before you're comfortable that you can help him or her. If you are confident you can help, then, in all probability, he or she will be able to help you. If you gradually find that only one minor segment lends itself to helping you both, keep the person as a "friends of the firm," but remove them from your PRS.

As we have seen, Level IIB is an important step in creating the mindshare you want. As we have noted in previous chapters, clarity in the utility of what you and your candidate do and with whom you both do it for is very important to getting the mindshare you both will want.

If your due diligence convinces you that your markets and market segments properly align, and you feel confident you can help your candidate, you're ready to proceed to Level IIA.

Level IIA – Does The Person Have PIP?

After clearing the Level IIB hurdle and deciding you and the other person are in a position to help each other, the relationship has ripened to red. Like the tomato, it is ready to pick.

At this point, you might think you're in good shape to form a great Level I relationship. Not so fast! You face a difficult step. You now have good personal rapport and know the person is "in your wheelhouse" of markets and market segments. But, for these relationships to flourish, you must make sure the person has **PIP**—that is, they are **P**urposeful, **I**ntentional, and **P**assionate about what they do.

As we discussed in Chapter 2 about branding, **PIP** relates to commitment. As you get to know Level I candidates and their businesses, listen closely to how they talk about their lives. Do they light up when they share about their business, how it's doing, and where it's going? Do they pull you into their world as they speak about plans for taking their business to the next level and better serving their clients? If so, they're showing you they are purposeful, intentional, and passionate about what they do, why they do it, and who they do it for. They have PIP!

On the other hand, if they talk in a way that suggests a business is only a means to an end (such as paying bills) or you start sensing burnout, then beware. This is a person who's probably living in survival mode rather than actively creating their lives with passion. And that's an indication they won't commit to a relationship with you.

Choosing people with PIP is critical to your relationship system. **If you sense a lack of purpose and passion in an individual, don't take the next PRS step.** I have seen many situations like this create heartburn for my clients, because they're not receiving what they expected. It's tough to walk away, because you get along with this person and they are in your wheelhouse—which, naturally, makes you think they will make for a good Level I relationship. But, continuing with the due diligence process here might ferret out "flakes": people who are late for meetings, cancel at the last minute, and fail to follow up as promised, to name a few shortcomings. Don't stress! Just let it go. Simply accept the situation for what it is. Don't delude yourself into thinking the person will change. And don't second-guess the gut. Move on!

Because you have had many interactions with your Level II candidate, you've been able to observe them in action. The key here is to give specific attention to the Level IIA criteria and make the proper assessment. Once you are convinced that your candidates have **PIP** and you can depend on them to do what they say they will do, you're ready to convert these relationships to Level I, if you choose.

Level I Relationship –
Committing To Helping Each Other Get A Result

At this stage, you should feel optimistic about the chances of formalizing a mutually beneficial referrer or "distributor" relationship with your candidates. You've done the necessary work to determine if you and these people are simpatico and are in a position to help one another. Now, it's time to enjoy the fruits (and tomato is a fruit) of your labor, right? Maybe. Maybe not.

Just because your candidates made it through the Level II process doesn't mean they can automatically be called a Level I relationship. There's one step remaining. Being at Level I requires personal meetings, specific conversations, and affirmative responses. In short, Level I requires the creation of an oral contract with each other. This explicit agreement is important, so that you both understand the responsibilities and accountabilities of the relationship to make it work.

Let's assume I have taken Sue, who is an accountant, through a Level II process. She has PIP and she has passed the other Level II hurdles. I have decided that today is the day for conversion. I'll ask her if she would like to be in a Level I relationship with me. We've agreed to meet for breakfast to discuss other issues and to get caught up. During breakfast, we are having a nice conversation and I decide the time is right to offer the "proposal," which is an explicit summary of a Level I relationship. Here's what I might say:

"Sue, it's occurred to me that you and I have had a real opportunity to get to know one another and to understand each other's business and clients. I'd like to tell you that I am thinking of you all the time, but unfortunately, that's not the case. Like you, I am spinning a lot of plates and there is a lot going on.

But I had this idea and I thought I would run it by you. I was thinking that it might make sense for us to meet once a month for a quick cup of coffee, 30 minutes at most, and brainstorm. Just maybe, I may have come across a person or situation during the month that I did not think about at the time, but that could be helpful to you. My thought is if we could help each other with one significant event over the course of the next year, it might make a real difference in both of our businesses. Would you be up for doing something like that?"

A Level I conversion conversation like this tends to elicit an immediate positive response every time. Why? Because it's short and sweet and asks very little of the individual—**just a monthly half-hour meeting with an expressed purpose: helping each other with one significant event over the course of a year.** This proposal is also comforting in that you're offering unsolicited support to the other person—you're saying you want to help them build their business, a task they're likely doing now completely on their own. This partnership you're proposing—and the specific goal of making a significant event happen—feels good to both of you!

The significant event you're suggesting would be either a referral to a direct client or a referral to another referral source who could potentially generate multiple referrals. Both situations could be significant. Because of the deeper and expressly committed nature of this relationship, the probability of multiple significant events is high. Still, it isn't wise to put pressure on the relationship to produce anything more than the yearly commitment. **Any expectation to do more than the yearly commitment pressures the relationship in a negative way.**

Immediately after Sue says yes to my proposal, I respond with: "Sue, let's get a standing date on the calendar." (We both pull out our digital calendars or appointment books.) Then I ask, "How about the second Tuesday of each month from 7:30 a.m. to 8:00 a.m.?"

When you get a positive response to a repeating day and time, then you both put that appointment on your calendars for the next twelve months. Why write it on your calendars immediately? Because this action solidifies the commitment and the result you both want. **It makes the relationship intentional.** As you both approach the scheduled meeting day, you review your calendars for the past 30 days to see what activities or people you've met that might help in the relationship. Because you've agreed to keep your meeting to thirty minutes (or whatever timeframe you've chosen), you'll want to be prepared and ready to offer your best information.

So, let's review the process.

The Level II due diligence process includes the following actions:

- Look for viable candidates and "score" each of them on ten personal characteristics. Then, take each prospective candidate through the vetting process, advancing only if/ when they pass each of three pre-Level I hurdles. If they fail to clear a hurdle, remove them from your PRS.

- Level IIC - Get to know a prospective candidate on a personal level.

- Level IIB - Determine if the candidate is playing in the same sandbox as you.

- Level IIA - Confirm that the candidate has PIP and integrity.

- Have an explicit conversation (i.e., set the stage for a Level I relationship).

- Level I – Make an agreement to help each other with one significant event in the next year.

- Schedule appointments to meet once a month for thirty minutes.

- Follow through on all agreements.

Now that I've walked you through the process of taking someone to a Level I relationship, let me ask you this very important question: What do you think the probability will be that Sue and I will help each other achieve that one significant event of giving each other a direct referral or a referral source?

Based on my experience with hundreds of service professionals who take this seriously by following the steps without taking shortcuts, it's a solid 100 percent. The only way it will not happen is if Sue's life or career changes significantly or if mine does.

When you take someone through the PRS process, you send a very strong message that you are there to help them succeed. Your brand in their eyes becomes very strong. Do you think once I create a Level I relationship with Sue I have to worry about my competition with her? Absolutely not! With Sue, I have made my competition irrelevant. The same is true for Sue's competition with me. We have both strengthened our brands in each other's eyes. Sue and I are committed to the result we both want. We have become distributors for each other!

Put another way, do you think I'm in the number one position in terms of mindshare with Sue? Of course! **The good news is that the short meeting we have each month strengthens mindshare so that it stays very strong.** You never want to make the mistake of not meeting with a Level I relationship each month, because meeting reinforces your number one mindshare position. I have seen situations in the past where individuals decided that, because they knew someone well, they didn't need to meet, so their interaction with the person decreased. Listen up: **The moment you start skipping meetings, mindshare begins to weaken.** You have lots of competitors out there who are knocking on the door of this person and would love to take your place. Don't assume just because you have known your Level I awhile that this can't happen to you.

Your meeting each month will give you a great deal of information about what is going on with your Level I relationship. For example, is it getting stronger? Do you seem to be building any business momentum? Do you feel energized after meeting? You will get to observe the person's body language and sense their attitude, which will offer you information about the progress you're making together. Coming to the meeting each month prepared to offer something that could be helpful to the other party will go a long way to having them work hard for you. It reinforces their decision to partner with you and reinforces the mutual commitment to help each other make that one significant event happen within a year—if not sooner!

Here is a visual to help you better understand the process of getting someone to a Level I relationship.

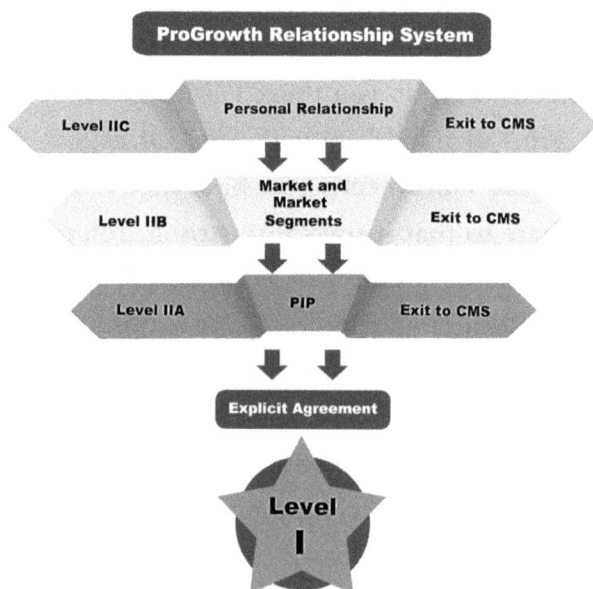

My hope is that you now have a clear understanding of how a well-managed relationship system can make a profound difference in your business. The illustration below drives this point home. While client referrals are always the best referrals because they have experienced your work and you have achieved mindshare with them, they are far and few between for most service profes-

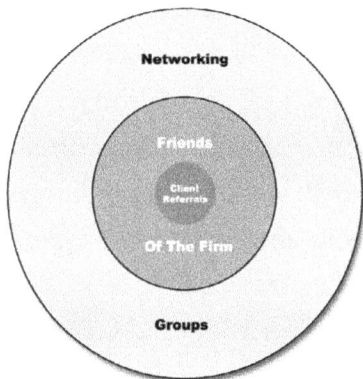

sionals. The further you get away from the bull's-eye, the less chance of any mindshare taking place. Service professionals in the outermost circle are depending upon the randomness of networking and the hope that some of the "friends of the firm" will come through for them.

A relationship system can make all the difference in helping you get the referrals you want to reach your business goals. As the next illustration clearly shows, it expands the bull's-eye to create more opportunity to get the referrals you want. You still have access to your "friends of the firm," but are less dependent on them and on networking. This frees up more time to work with committed referrers and on client matters, which will yield stronger business results for you.

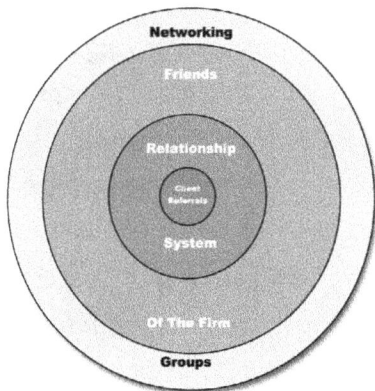

Converting A Level II Relationship To Level 3

As we discussed earlier, you may occasionally form a close and personal relationship with an individual you respect and trust. Usually, these relationships develop over a number of years. As a Level II candidate, they are unable to qualify as a Level I relationship, because your market segments and theirs are not properly aligned.

For example, let's assume that you and I have known each other for twenty years and we both are involved in the retail industry. You're working with big-box companies, such as Nordstrom's, Macy's, and Saks Fifth Avenue. I, on the other hand, am working with small boutique shops. While we are both working within the retail market, our market segments are significantly different. We clearly cannot have a Level I relationship with each other.

However, because of our long-time personal relationship and the fact that we are operating in a similar market, we both agree to look out for each other. To formalize this, I must have an explicit conversation to convert you to a Level 3 and request your agreement. That conversation would go something like this:

"Mark, as you know we're both in the retail market, but our market segments are vastly different. The chances of my being able to clearly help you are unlikely. Even so, because of our long term personal relationship, I was thinking it might be a good idea for us to get together once a quarter and update each other on our activities. It's possible that during that period I'll come across a person or situation that may be helpful to you. Over the course of the year, we might even be able to help each other with one significant event, like a direct introduction to a potential client, or an introduction to someone who has potential to create multiple referrals. Would you be open to this type of a relationship?"

Based on what I've seen in my experience as a coach, the individual will nod and say "yes"! Again, the moment the person does say "yes," you should both pull out your digital calendars and schedule four quarterly meetings. This creates the intention, and prompts the mutual follow-through that will make the meeting productive.

I need to emphasize once more that your primary goal is to convert Level II to Level I relationships. As your PRS develops, you want most of your focus to be on potential Level I relationships. **Any Level 3 relationships should be kept at a minimum, because those relationships are less likely to produce the results you want.**

Managing Your ProGrowth Relationship System (PRS)

Just as a company employs a well-managed distribution system to get its products into the hands of its customers, you must manage your relationship system to get the results you want for your business.

Since your relationship system is separate and distinct from your contact management system (CMS), it is important that you manage it separately. You will never have more than twenty or twenty-five people within your PRS. Individuals who are in your system are either going through the Level II "ripening tomato" process, are a Level I relationship, or are a Level 3 relationship. As a Level II candidate goes through the process, it's important to record your "touches," as well as the content of your meetings. Touches are any kind of contact, whether by phone, email, or in person that you might have with a Level II candidate or a Level I relationship, keeping in mind the most important touch is your "in person" meetings. You want to be able to make a good decision should you decide to convert a Level II to a Level I relationship. Documenting this information will also provide you with valuable feedback on how your PRS is performing.

To help you stay organized, set up your PRS in a spreadsheet. Sample column headings could include:

1. **Name** – The first and last name of people in your system

2. **Status** – The current relationship level of the individual (Level IIC, Level IIB, Level IIA, etc.)

3. **Touches** – Dates you reached out to that individual (make sure these occur at least once every 30 days)

4. **Notes** – Any comments or thoughts you took away from meetings, or communication that you had. It's information that helps form the basis for your decision whether to convert the individual to a Level I relationship.

Spending ten to twenty minutes a couple of times each week keeping your relationship system current can make all the difference in its performance for your business. Not keeping it up to date or recording your touches will negatively impact the results you want, because you're not staying on top of the information you need to make good decisions. Remember: This is your distribution system, and it must be given the attention it deserves in order to work for you.

As a purchaser of this book, you will have free access to the ProGrowth Premier website for three months. This is an effective, easy-to-use way to manage your PRS and plan for your professional and personal goals online. Our instruction videos will have you off to a quick start and help you better understand how to get the most out of your PRS. At the end of three months, you'll have the option of continuing to manage your system online with ProGrowth Premier (at a nominal cost), or switching to off-line management. See instructions at the back of the book to learn how to redeem your free three-month offer.

Now that you know you can make your competition irrelevant by capitalizing on the power of mindshare, let's continue moving forward. We'll begin by learning how to create a solid foundation for grabbing mindshare. The first step is to understand you have the ability to be a rainmaker. Part Two starts by revealing how to use your social style to create the all-important personal connections with others that start the process that can bring potential new business consistently.

PART TWO

The Foundation of Mindshare

In Part Two, we get to the heart of mindshare: what it means and how you cultivate it in a way that's authentic to who you are as an individual. We'll open with a discussion on how *you* can be an effective rainmaker by understanding your social style and using it as strength to connect with others. Next, we will take the vision you have for your business's future and create a doable three-year plan for making it reality. We then move into creating a tandem three-year plan for your personal goals that helps ensure YOU are on the front burner. To feel good professionally, you must be able to feel good personally, and vice versa. All three chapters are critical in laying a solid foundation for your mindshare positioning.

6

YOU ARE A RAINMAKER
It's Just A Matter Of Understanding

"Coming together is a beginning; keeping together is progress; working together is success."

-HENRY FORD

The first step in creating mindshare is connecting personally with another human being. Without this connection, nothing else happens. We typically make a connection on a personal level, based on our social style and our ability to understand the social styles of others. Connecting helps us get comfortable with one another, and sets the stage for a long-term relationship with the other person; in this case, with another service professional. Harnessing the power of connection, whatever your social style, is the key to becoming a rainmaker, or person who brings in new business.

Many believe that "rainmakers are born, not made." Recently, I was speaking with a managing partner of a large law firm who is convinced, along with his partners, that an individual either has the rainmaker personality, or doesn't. To him, a rainmaker is someone who is outgoing, gregarious, and has no reservations about striking up conversations with strangers at events. It's someone who has the uncanny ability to bring in clients by the sheer magnetism of his or her personality. So, does that mean if you don't have that outgoing personality, you *can't* be a rainmaker? Of course not!

As a service professional, you are always interacting with other people. It's the nature of your job. Interacting with people in a way that allows both parties to be comfortable is known as "rapport." Wikipedia defines rapport as "one of the most important features or characteristics of subconscious communication. It is commonality of perspective: being "in sync" with or "on the same wavelength" as the person with whom you are talking. There is no mention that you must somehow have this incredible outgoing personality to succeed. Establishing rapport simply means that you find a way to connect in spite of the differing social styles of the parties involved.

The first hurdle someone has to clear once you've brought them into your PRS is Level IIC, "Can You Establish Rapport?" This is all about being able to connect with the other person's social style. Over the years, I've helped many people who never saw themselves as rainmakers learn to use their social style to create great relationships with other professionals and build substantial practices. **The key is to be comfortable with who you are, and to use the strengths of your social style to communicate in a way that is helpful to the other person, given his or her social style may be very different from yours.**

Why? So much of what you do as a service professional is by interacting with other human beings. Again, mindshare does not begin to take place without a connection. That is why we take the time to make sure that we can develop a comfortable personal relationship with a Level IIC candidate. Communication is affected by the way you come across. If you try to be someone you're not (i.e., inauthentic), it will affect the way your message is communicated. At worst, it could create the impression that you're uncaring or distrustful. Being who you are has the highest probability of helping the other party feel comfortable. But you also need to be sensitive to who THEY are and understand how to interact with them. So, act naturally, but with sensitivity towards your audience. You literally have the power to shut down communication or to enhance it by using the strengths of your social style.

In my opinion, one of the simplest and best models for explaining the various social styles is the DISC Profile System™. DISC is an acronym for Dominance, Influence, Steadiness, and Conscientiousness. The DISC Profile System™ is a premier personality system that has been used around the world for over 50 years. The DISC Profile System™ can help you understand your own social style, and also help you understand the behavior style of others, whether they're clients or referral sources. This makes it a valuable behavioral tool for bridging communication gaps and facilitating rapport. The assessment itself only takes 10-15 minutes and the results are immediately available online through a very comprehensive report. If you'd like to take the DISC assessment, you can do so as a purchaser of this book at progrowth-premier.com at a reduced fee.

As the graphic on the next page indicates, the DISC Profile System™ is based on four social styles that describe an individual's behavior. These styles are identified by one of four quadrants, named for four personality factors: dominance, influence, steadiness, and compliance. The quadrants are defined by the intersection of two axes measuring opposite attributes. The axes are Assertiveness/Receptiveness and Control/Openness.

The DISC Profile™ System

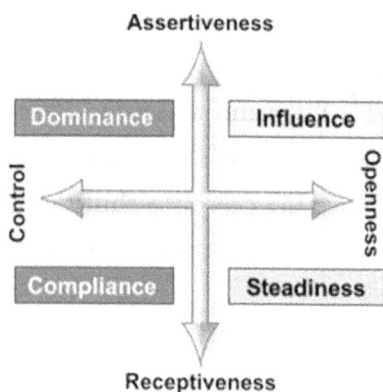

Assertiveness

Dominance | Influence

Control | Openness

Compliance | Steadiness

Receptiveness

The vertical axis is a continuum between the opposite attributes of Assertiveness and Receptiveness. At one end, you have **Assertive** people, who are proactive and direct. They would rather lead than follow, and find a way to take immediate action whenever they can. They are trailblazers who like to take advantage of opportunities and make their own way. At the other end of the continuum, you have **Receptive** people, who are fairly patient and typically very cautious. They usually like to avoid risk and dislike taking action on their own, unless there is a lot of pressure from a situation or person to do so.

The horizontal axis is a continuum between the opposite attributes of Control and Openness. At one end, you have **Controlling** people, who are practical and somewhat cynical. It is hard for them to accept situations at first glance, because they need facts and rational arguments. They don't reveal their cards very quickly, so it takes more time to understand them. At the other end of the continuum, you have **Open** people, who are usually very friendly and trusting. They like to wear their emotions on their shirtsleeve. You always have a good sense what they're thinking or feeling.

As the graphic shows, there are different degrees and combinations of these attributes, as reflected by a person's position within each quadrant.

Let's take a look at the four personality factors, which name the quadrants of DISC Profile System™: **Dominance**, **Influence**, **Steadiness**, and **Compliance**.

Dominance – "The Achiever" (D)

Dominant people, also known as "achievers" or "D's," tend to be driven and overachieving. They are usually very direct and assertive, and want to control people and situations. Entrepreneurs often fall into this group. They are independently minded, motivated to succeed, and will do whatever it takes to get their way! On the downside, D's are sometimes short with people, have bad tempers, and can get aggressive in certain situations when they are under pressure. They like controlling their environment and do not want to be controlled themselves. They are also results-oriented, very competitive, and have the ambition to succeed no matter what roadblocks are put in front of them. They thrive on challenges and rarely will back away, because their biggest fear is their own failure to achieve their standards. Individuals with this social style are not great at idle chitchat. They are not usually trusting of others and will often try to get things done on their own. Because they focus on winning, they are not too concerned about a win-win scenario. They much prefer that they win and, if you lose, they believe it's your fault, not theirs!

As you might expect, Dominants do not make the best team players. Should you come up against someone who displays these characteristics, focus on them—because, as far as they're concerned, it *is* all about them. Encouraging these people to talk about their successes and accomplishments is a good way to get them comfortable with you. If you want to endear yourself to them, identify their issues and then focus on the potential results that might help their cause. They like people who can analyze quickly and come up with solutions. They also like people who display competence and common sense. They may quickly try and intimidate you with their assertiveness, and will judge you based on how you stand up to them both in terms of your confidence and influence.

If you are a Dominant person, recognize that you must be patient when dealing with others. You process things very quickly and you like to get to the bottom line. You can come across as uncaring, not very empathetic and not very interested in the other person. Give others their time to be understood. Rushing to where you want the relationship to go will scare people off because they will think that all you want is what you can get from them. Learn to be a great listener. It is ok to influence the conversation, but you must give others their time to fully share their arguments even if you disagree with them. As you get to know others, find ways to help so that you gain their confidence. Mindshare will not begin to take place unless a person is comfortable with who you are and believes that you care about them.

A former coaching client of mine, we'll call him "Bob," is a very bright attorney who thrives on winning every case he litigates. He is a hard charger and has a great deal of confidence in his abilities. He is a member of a large law firm and competes with other top notch members of the firm for visibility and contribution to the firm's revenues. Bob was referred to me because, while he is a great litigator, he had problems sustaining a practice with his own client following. I was told that he was short with people and not very engaging. That information told me that Bob probably had a strong Dominant social style. On the day I met with Bob, I went to the firm and was shown to his office by his administrative assistant. As I walked through the door, his assistant announced my name. Bob was working at his desk and barely lifted his head to acknowledge me. Immediately, I knew that I was in for an interesting conversation. I introduced myself, stuck out my hand, and waited for him to shake it. He never got out of his chair, but motioned for me to have a seat in one of the chairs in front of his expansive desk. Clearly, he was already trying to position himself as the person with the power through his intimidation techniques.

When I was earning my MBA from Pepperdine University, I had an organizational behavior professor that I respected tremendously. I learned a great deal from him about human behavior. One of the most important things he taught me was that "It is okay to respond but not to react." Sometimes, you will come up against an individual who causes you to want to react in a way that will only fuel the situation. It is best, in these cases, to respond but not react, so emotions don't interfere with communication.

There was no question I needed to apply that here. Bob wanted to show me that he was a powerful person. As soon as I sat down, he immediately said, "What are you going to do for me?" in a rather gruff and cocky voice. Talk about being bottom-line driven! Without reacting, I simply looked him in the eye, paused, and responded calmly, "I'm not going to do anything for you. If we work together, *you* are going to *do* for you, with my help."

At that point, my sense was that Bob was either going to throw me out or realize that he could not intimidate me for his own purposes. He started to let down his guard, and we began to communicate at the same level. We went on to have a very good conversation about him and his practice. I actually think he felt relieved that he did not need to be the power broker. I shared with him how he would work together, and that we would be a team to get him where he wanted to go. In essence, I gave him permission not to have a need to intimidate or bully me, so that we could work well together. He was comfortable that we would be results-oriented, and that I would serve his best interests.

Our experience working together gave Bob the confidence he needed to develop real relationships with other professionals. Today, Bob is very successful and has a thriving law practice. He still has a results-oriented social style, but he has become much more patient with people. Most importantly, he has learned that not everyone sees life through the same kaleidoscope of life he does—and he has learned to adjust his social style accordingly, in order to help others feel comfortable and hence, gain their trust.

Influence – "The Socializer" (I)

Influencer people, also known as "socializers" or "I's," are enthusiastic, optimistic, and very outgoing. They like to take action, and encourage collaboration. In addition, I's really enjoy working with people, and take care not to offend others. They're very good communicators and socially confident. Because they are rather talkative, they sometimes embellish on impulse, because they have an urge to relate or impress those around them.

Not surprisingly, socializers don't deal well with rejection. They want to be very open with other people, and will sometimes share information or express feelings that others might find too revealing. Because they are optimists and exude enthusiasm, however, people will typically view their openness as positive. By creating a motivational environment, Influencers want to make sure that all participants are comfortable. They will generally look at the good in people. They will trust people until they have a reason not to trust them. While I's are good at seeing the big picture, they are at times not very good at hands-on management and details. They depend on their outgoing personality to get them where they want to go, which sometimes creates challenges for keeping their business on track. You may have met people along the way who you felt might make great referral sources, only to find out they were nothing more than a good talker. At the time, they were legitimately very interested in you, but as soon as you both went your separate ways, they were on to other people. It is probably because they are good at "being in the moment," but not so good at following up.

One of my past clients, who we'll call "Fred," is a wealth management advisor. Fred came to me because he operates in a highly competitive environment and wanted to grow his book of business more quickly. There was no question he had an Influencer type social style and that he was matched very well with the type of business that he was in. Once I started to work with him, however, I began to see a pattern where he would commit to do things by our next session, and then show up with nothing done. As I got to know Fred, it was clear that he really wanted to please, but could not come through as he had committed. He just was not good at following through. My sense was that, as he developed relationships, it wasn't long before people labeled him a "flake."

Mindshare occurs because someone feels there is a mutual commitment. Without commitment, the perception becomes, "This guy is all talk and no substance." Naturally, this taints the brand, which kills the chance for mindshare. When I brought these observations to Fred's attention, he admitted that, while he wanted to keep his commitments to people, he simply couldn't seem to make it happen. As a result, any potential mindshare and relationships would begin to wane.

Fred and I spent a great deal of our time together focusing on time management. He had been trying to be all things to people and found himself overcommitting because he never wanted to say "no" to anyone—he wanted to say "yes" all the time and make people feel good! We concentrated on making sure that Fred let go of his unproductive relationships and time wasting activities so he could live up to his important commitments without overextending himself. We also used his digital calendar to make appointments with himself and to ensure he prioritized objectives and deadlines. These small changes made all the difference in helping Fred keep his promises and not take on more than he could handle.

Today, Fred feels much better about himself. He is highly regarded and has built a substantial practice focusing on the right relationships where he can truly add value. Understanding his social style helped him make critical corrections. Now he is in control of his time and commitments, thereby enhancing his credibility with clients and referral sources. This ultimately improved his brand, which gave him a better opportunity to develop mindshare.

Remember, understanding your own social style and that of others, will help you engage because you are genuinely interested in how you make them feel. When you are in a conversation with an Influencer, get them to talk about their friends or other people (in a positive way). Encourage them to share what they do outside of work. Remember, they are socializers. So, inquiring about anything related to people or group activities will help the two of you connect.

Compliance/Conscientiousness/Control
"The Meticulous One" (C)

Compliance people, also known as "conscientious" or "controller" types, or "C's," are typically reserved and controlling. They are analytical and look at things in a very systematic way. Also, they tend to be fairly private, and feel uncomfortable revealing too much about themselves. Their biggest fear is getting it wrong or being criticized for not doing something in a methodical way. On a related note, C's have a hard time with people who are the opposite of them—i.e., who just "slap it against the wall and hope something sticks." They will work hard for a client who appreciates the attention to detail.

C's are meticulous. Their most significant limiting tendencies are to overanalyze things (think "paralysis through analysis") and to isolate themselves too much. If you are dealing with a person like this and want to develop mindshare, the best way to create rapport is to find common ground when discussing their situation and to do so in a focused way, without a lot of extraneous chitchat. People with this social style like using their knowledge and expertise to solve problems. Simply asking, "How would you address that issue"? during a discussion gives them permission to systematically share how they might deal with something. That conversation then begins to pull them out of their shell, and encourages them to feel more comfortable with you. They get to talk about something they know, and do not have to worry about being wrong.

I will never forget working with a client we'll call "Phil," who'd been a CPA for ten years and had a small book of business. When we first got together, it was difficult to even have a conversation. While he was gracious, he was so reserved and found it difficult to express his thoughts. It seemed that he analyzed everything over and over in his mind, which made it hard for him to articulate anything! In fact, each time Phil would try to explain a concept or idea, he'd grab a whiteboard and create a schematic to illustrate his thinking. In all of this, it was clear that he enjoyed solving problems and liked to visualize them, so he could look at all of the issues.

When it came to relationships, Phil admitted he found it very difficult to go to networking functions to meet people; he just wasn't comfortable with the small talk. Given his social style, I understood why that type of environment wasn't his thing. But, despite the fact he found the functions challenging, he agreed it was important to attend them, so he could meet others who might become good referral sources for him.

In order to get him to feel comfortable, I suggested that he go to those events with a different mindset: He would look forward to meeting people and helping them solve an issue. Armed with this approach, Phil would feel more positive about the experience. Simply being more positive would help him come across in a much more favorable way with others.

Since Phil found it difficult to initiate conversations, I suggested that he introduce himself and allow the other person to initiate the dialogue. Once the conversation began to flow, asking questions and getting the other person to talk about him- or herself and his or her business was a perfect way for Phil to use his social style to connect. Asking questions not only gets the other party to talk, but feeds Phil's comfort level, because he is used to asking questions to do one of his favorite things: problem-solving! And, if Phil is conversing with a Dominant social style, that individual will appreciate him all the more, since he is zeroing in on specific issues. Similarly, if Phil were dealing with an Influencer social style, that person would *really* appreciate the interest Phil was taking and the fact he's letting them talk—since talking is exactly what Influencers like to do!

Steadiness/Conformity
"The Accommodator" (S)

Individuals with the Steadiness/Conformity social style, also known as "accommodators" or "S's," are usually fairly even-tempered and conformist. They are very patient and like to accommodate people they work with. Because they don't get ruffled, S's are usually very tactful and humble in their approach with others. They get along with most people because they like to go with the flow. Individuals with this social style typically do not like to see a lot of change in their life or in their work. In fact, they are fairly slow at adapting to any kind of change, because it disrupts their normal routine. They have a normal way of doing things, which can be problematic and prevent them from meeting deadlines. They are more concerned about making sure everything is done properly than being on time.

A person with this social style has worked hard to develop very specialized skills. There are many lawyers and accountants who are S's. They enjoy helping others and are very loyal to those they work with. Plus, they are very good at listening to their clients. They can usually take a difficult situation involving a client or an adversary and create a harmonious environment, so that the parties calm down and work together. Since S's don't like conflict, they are very good at minimizing it. They take pride in doing great work for their clients, and appreciate being acknowledged for it.

Because of their methodical approach, S's need to surround themselves with people who can make decisions quickly and will push them to get outside their comfort zone and prioritize issues based on urgency.

My experience over the years with S-dominant individuals is that they are wonderful people who really care—but who are more interested in the work they do than in bringing in new clients. It reminds me of a client of mine we'll call "Susan," who is a very good lawyer and is highly regarded in her firm for her legal acumen. Unfortunately, Susan did not have her own clients, and found it difficult and uncomfortable to do the necessary work to bring in any to the firm. Given the type of firm she was in, Susan knew that she would need to develop a stable of clients to contribute to the long-term economic growth of her firm if she ever wanted to make partner.

Susan was referred to me for help with her situation. In our very first conversation, she admitted she was very uncomfortable with the thought of going out to try and bring in business. She felt that she went to law school so that she could practice law and do good work for clients. In her mind, "drumming up business" was like being a salesperson, which felt demeaning. Susan had a very pleasant demeanor, and I could tell I was dealing with a classic Steadiness/Conformity social style.

In working with Susan, I didn't want to rush her into doing all the things that made her uncomfortable. We started off instead with little things that were *in* her comfort zone. One of the things that I asked her to do was to view herself not as a lawyer, but as an owner of a business that provides legal services. As the owner, Susan had to understand how to position the business strategically and operationally. She also had to understand how to market the business and how to capture her clients in a predictable way. I had her visualize her name on the door, which meant the success of the business was her responsibility. This was a good start for us, because it took Susan out of the realm of technician and into the mindset of a business owner. As we worked together, I could see that her confidence was growing.

Susan knew that I was right there with her, which provided the safety of knowing that she was not going down this path alone. Once she started developing a few of her own clients, she became very excited about being able to do great work for them. Even more exciting was knowing they were *her* clients, and not just "work" that was handed to her by someone else. The key in Susan's case was to make sure that she was comfortable at every step, so that she was able to strengthen her confidence and continue moving forward.

If you interact with an "accommodator," you will enjoy their company. You will also quickly learn that they are loyal, hard-working individuals who enjoy talking about their families. It takes S's a little while to warm up to people, but once they do, you can rest assured they are "all in." As a result, S's make very good Level I relationships. If they tell you they are going to do something, they will get it done—and on time. Since they enjoy being acknowledged for their hard work, your show of appreciation will go a long way.

The importance of establishing rapport cannot be overemphasized. It is a critical first step in any meaningful relationship It is important to know that many of us land firmly in one social style, yet most if us have "shadows" of other social styles. One person may be a strong D with leanings toward I or C.. These are nuances you can learn with practice. The more you practice, the more effective you will be at engaging others.

To be able to connect with another person by developing a strong rapport means everything when it comes to your brand developing a strong mindshare position. Being able to understand the four social styles and how to successfully interact with them is one of the well-kept secrets that will give you a significant competitive advantage over others—and will unlock your ability to be a rainmaker. If you have never taken the DISC assessment, I highly recommend you do so. It's definitely a worthwhile investment of your time.

Now that you see you *can* be a fabulous rainmaker, let's move on to better understanding how to use these newfound skills to build the business you want. In the next chapter, we will put together your vision and plan to make it happen. Let's do it!

7

YOUR PROFESSIONAL GOALS
Know Your Target And How You'll Hit It

"The secret of achievement is to hold a picture of a successful outcome in mind"

—*HENRY DAVID THOREAU*

Once you've made a connection with someone, you need to begin laying the foundation so that mindshare can take place. Earlier, we discussed the importance of the strength of your brand in creating mindshare. If you recall, 20% of your brand value is based on the utility of what you do, who you do it for, and why you do it. In this chapter, we will be focusing on creating a vision for your business and then a game plan for making it happen. By the end of the chapter, you will see how and why having a vision and knowing how to execute it is one of the secrets to for having a strong mindshare position.

We have established that you are both a brand and a business. I think, at this point, you get that people are going to do business with you *because* of you. Since you are a business as well as CEO of that business, it is important that you clearly understand what your goals are and how you'll achieve them. That understanding will go a long way in helping you strengthen your brand and ultimately gain a strong mindshare position.

Your Vision

The first thing you need to do is to picture the type of business that you we want. There is an old adage, "If the mind can perceive it, the body can achieve it."

Visualization has been the key for many successful people. It is about willing yourself to create a picture of what you would like to do and then making it happen. A good example of this would be visualizing a shot in golf before you address the ball to hit it. The great Jack Nicklaus said that he never hit a shot, not even in practice, without having a very sharp, in-focus picture of it in his head. He said he would first see the ball where he wanted to finish. He would then see the ball going there, its trajectory and shape, even its behavior on landing. He then would picture himself making the kind of swing that would actually make those images become reality. Only then would he address the ball, let his body swing the club, and hit the shot his mind created. We all know the kind of success he achieved.

In her book *The Secret*, Rhonda Byrne uses visualization as one of the major tenets to living the life you want. Many people have used this technique to do amazing things. It doesn't cost anything to implement: The only thing it requires is a commitment to make the results you want happen.

Jack Canfield, in his book, *The Success Principles*, talks about the importance of taking 100% responsibility for your life. He devotes very specific chapters to topics such as being clear on why you're here, deciding what you want, believing it's possible and, most importantly, believing in yourself.

One cannot underestimate the power of visualization. When you can see and feel the success that you want, you are much more likely to make it happen. You also will be more passionate, because you have a purpose—a fact that will be obvious to the people you encounter.

So, what about you? What is the vision for your business? If you and I were sitting here three years from today and you were thrilled with what you had accomplished in your business, what would that look like and feel like to you? Let's build that vision together.

THE VISION FOR YOUR BUSINESS

For the purposes of this example, let's assume you are a commercial insurance producer who works for a regional or national insurance brokerage house. (You can apply the same principles to your own discipline as we go through this example.)

Your Income

Like any business, the overall objective is to make a profit. As service professionals, the bottom-line is our income. So, the first question then is, "How much personal income do you want to put in your pocket and take home by the end of year three? The exciting thing about creating this vision of the future you want is that you don't have any constraints. The primary consideration should be where you are in your career and what the overall economy is like with respect to your discipline. If you made $75,000 this year and want to make $500,000 in the third year of your plan, that might be pie-in-the-sky type thinking, unless your discipline is on fire and there are potential clients waiting in line! Let's say for this exercise you made $125,000 this year and decide that you would like to make $250,000 in year three. That's realistic, but will require hard work and focus to achieve it.

Amount Of Revenue You Need To Create The Income You Want

The next question is, "How much revenue will you need to bring into your firm in order to make the income you have targeted? Let's assume that you are on a 40% split of commissions with your firm, and the 60% the firm gets includes your expenses. That would mean that you need to generate $625,000 in total commissions to net $250,000 in personal income.

Okay! So far, we know that you want our business to produce $250,000 in income for you, and we know that it will take $625,000 in gross commissions to get there. Now, the next thing that we have to understand is where the commissions will come from. Who do the clients look like and how much revenue would you expect from each client?

Who Are The Clients That Will Create The Revenue?

Your Markets

Once the commission levels are established, it's important for you to understand where it will come from. **The first step is to establish the clients you want to work with.** What <u>markets</u> are they in? A market is typically defined as a set of all of the actual or potential buyers of a product or service. Examples of a market are: manufacturing, distribution, high net worth individuals, service companies, etc. **It is best if you choose appropriate markets based on your present experience, as well as any emerging market you feel presents strong opportunities.**

Let's say that you identify three markets you want to focus on. They are:

1. Manufacturing

2. Distribution

3. Construction

You decide that, based on your experience and overall market conditions, you want 40% of the total commissions coming from manufacturing ($250,000), 30% from distribution ($187,500), and 30% from construction companies ($187,500).

Your Market Segments

Your next step is to identify what <u>market segment</u> within each one of those markets you want your future clients to come from. This is an extremely important exercise, as it will not only help you clearly understand where you are going to acquire your clients, but will also create great clarity for those with whom you want to develop strong mindshare. **The market segment should be very specific in terms of geography, description, and average revenue you expect to generate** on an annual basis for each client with those characteristics.

Identifying the appropriate market segment is key. Remember the guy who said, "I work with middle-market manufacturers"? We agreed that this individual was going to find it difficult to create any kind of mindshare because of the lack of clarity he had about the type of clients he worked with. When targeting manufacturers as a market, keep in mind the size of a manufacturer can vary from a garage-based operation doing $100,000 a year to a large multinational manufacturer doing billions of dollars a year. **In picking the appropriate market segment, it's important that you take into account your experience and the resources that you bring to bear to service that client.** If you attempt to go too large; your competitors could squish you. If you go too small, you may not be able to generate the margins you need in order for your business to be profitable.

I cannot overemphasize the importance of having a well-defined market segment. It conveys a significant amount of information to the individuals who may have the ability to refer clients to you. The average approximate revenue you expect to generate based on the target client you have identified is important because it will not only help you understand how many clients you will need to achieve your market goal revenue figure, but will also help you stay within the market segments you have identified and avoid wasting time with the wrong prospects. Presumably, if your average revenue per client is higher, your clients have more complex issues than a small client needing fewer services. If you consistently acquire clients outside of the market segment and they're not able to achieve the average anticipated revenue you need and deserve, it will impact your revenue and ultimately your income. Because of the resources you and your firm bring to bear, these clients are clearly too small to benefit from the services that you can perform.

Now that we have an understanding of the importance of clearly identifying the target clients we want, let's define how you will articulate their profile to yourself and others:

1. *Manufacturers* - privately-owned companies in Southern California who have been in business for at least five years, are profitable and doing between $5 million and

$50 million in revenue. They typically will have between 50 and 250 employees. The company will specialize in consumer goods or technology products. The average revenue per client is $35,000.

2. *Distributors* – privately-owned companies in Southern California that have been in business for at least five years, have between 50 and 150 employees, with operations in multiple states, are profitable and are doing between $5 million and $50 million in revenue. Average revenue per client is $30,000.

3. *Contractors* – General Contractors based in Southern California, who specialize in residential construction for large developers and are doing $10 million to $100 million in revenue. Involved in multi-state projects and have approximately 250 employees. Average revenue per client is $50,000.

Do we have complete clarity? Definitely! If someone were to ask you what type of clients you work with, you'd be able to respond without hesitation: "I work with three types of clients and they look like this…" **Being able to describe your clients makes the "who do you do it for" component of your brand crystal clear to potential referrers and helps you stay focused on the type of business you need. This is extremely empowering for you.**

The average revenue per client is confidential information to you and is not shared with others. It tells you the activity you will need to hit your numbers. Based on the average revenue per client you are looking for in each market, you will need to acquire approximately <u>seven manufacturing clients</u>, <u>six distributor clients</u>

and <u>four contractor clients</u> to achieve your revenue objectives in order to develop the income you want.

Your Relationship System To Capture The Clients

In Chapter 4, "A Distribution System Is A Must," we talked about the importance of a distribution system to a business. For service professionals, our distribution system is our relationship system: the individuals who we call **Level I** relationships. These are the people for whom we are in the number one mindshare position and who we can absolutely depend on to help us capture the clients we want.

So you might ask, "How many Level I relationships should I develop?" My experience over the years has been that **if you can develop just fifteen Level I relationships over a three-year period, there is a high probability you will hit your target numbers.** Why fifteen? That number has proven to be the optimum number of relationships that you can develop and manage properly. Your goal is to make your business more predictable, right? If you are active in the marketplace, you will likely get those random referrals along the way, but we want to move the needle to a more predictable outcome. We do not want to rely on a strategy of "hope."

If you have done your homework and have taken the individuals through the "*ripening tomato process*" we discussed in Chapter 5 on the ProGrowth Relationship System (PRS), you will see a significant impact on your business. In each Level I relationship, you will be in the number one mindshare position. No matter how challenging the competitive environment might be, you will be able to make your competition irrelevant with these individuals.

I know you may be thinking that spending 7 ½ hours a month on your distribution/relationship system (thirty minutes with fifteen Level I's, not including drive time) sounds like too much.

I can only offer you this: What if it were a total commitment of fifteen hours per month? Are you better off investing this time *knowing* you're going to produce tangible results, or would you be better off investing the same amount of time attending networking functions, where the results will be sketchy at best? I'm hoping at this point you agree that Level I interaction is a very good investment of your precious time. **You are investing the time because of the significant impact it can have on your business.**

Strengthening Your Brand

The environment for almost all service professionals of various disciplines is extremely competitive. It's important that you have a branding strategy in order to stand out from the crowd. Some ideas might include writing articles, giving speeches, using social media, or sending out monthly email broadcasts. Here is some more information about each:

Writing Articles/Blogs—Publishing an article or a blog positions you as an expert and someone who keeps current on relevant issues. Doing an article/blog once a month, or even quarterly, will help you get greater exposure in your marketplace and will definitely strengthen your brand.

Giving speeches—Speaking to groups is always a good way to help your audience understand who you are and regard you as an expert in your industry. People will appreciate your business acumen and your passion for what you do—both very important qualities for strengthening your brand and developing mindshare. Typically, the speeches will be to others who may have the opportunity to refer you. Giving speeches once a quarter keeps your name out in the marketplace.

Social media—Having an ongoing presence in the various social media outlets is another way to keep your name and the name of the firm out in front. Again, having people see how you (who are synonymous with your brand) stay on top of the issues in your profession is a great way to build mindshare. The important thing is to do it continuously. For planning purposes, you might want to update weekly to remain top of mind. Being active in social media takes a little time, but the exposure can become significant for you in the long run.

Email broadcast—One of the best ways to stay in front of all the people in both your contact management system and relationship system is with a monthly email broadcast (not to be confused with a "blast," which is less targeted and considered spam.) Typically, this is a short two- or three-line message on some issue that is particularly relevant and/or timely for your discipline. Never make it any longer than a few sentences, because people won't read it—they're busy and will just end up hitting delete. People will, however, give you five seconds—particularly if you're offering a quick read that is helpful to them. As an example, let's assume that an article crosses your desk involving updates on the workers compensation law in your state. These updates could potentially impact businesses. You send out your monthly email broadcast and it reads, "This month, the Worker's Compensation Board issued new rules relative to workers compensation and what employers must do to meet the requirements. To view these updated regulations, please click this link which will send you to the full update." Bull's-eye! You've provided value (and put your name in front of the reader) with a short, informative touch that doesn't intrude on anyone's time.

By the third year, if you are regularly contacting 200 to 300 people or more through your branding strategy, you'll likely be realizing a significant ROI. Remember, you're *only* contacting people you know or met along the way. **Do not make it a spamming effort to people you don't know. Spamming will only create negative publicity for your brand.** On a related note, always provide people you email the ability to opt out. And, never end an email with "If I can help you, please give me a call." That turns an informative piece into a sales piece—which negates the impact you want to have. Don't worry; if someone likes what you wrote and wants to talk to you, they'll be in touch!

Through email broadcasts, you position yourself as an expert who stays on top of the issues. More importantly, by touching people monthly, you are strengthening mindshare and triggering the likelihood that someone will want to talk to you about a specific matter or a potential client. My clients who have faithfully sent out monthly emails receive a lot of positive feedback. That reaction is priceless—especially for something that takes only minutes to do each month!

The lesson to be learned here? **Always keep your eyes and ears open for brand-strengthening activities that are time-efficient and effective.**

For the purposes of this exercise, let's assume you have decided to do the following four activities:

1. Write one article a quarter.

2. Give a speech twice a year to CPA groups on managing risk.

3. Do weekly updates on LinkedIn, Facebook and Twitter.

4. Send an email broadcast once a month to a select distribution list.

Other Issues That Could Affect Your Business

In the event you are a solo practitioner or a partner in a smaller firm, you may have other business issues that you would like to include in your plan. These may include strategic, personnel, financial, or operational issues that are specific to your operation. Since you are a commercial insurance broker with a regional or national firm in this example, you probably will not need to deal with these issues, as your corporate office takes care of them. However, let's take a look at each of them anyway, so you can have a good idea how they might impact your business if you are a solo practitioner or a partner in a smaller firm.

Strategic Decisions

These issues are usually at the "20,000-foot level," above and beyond normal day-to-day operations. They are typically broad policy questions or other challenges that can affect the longer-term growth and direction of the firm. It will usually involve the firm's mission, its values, and its clients. As an example, a strategic decision could be that you decide by the end of the third year that you want to have two additional partners and three new offices to continue the growth of your firm.

Personnel Decisions

People are your greatest asset in a service business. In order to maintain your service levels, you may want to consider adding people to ensure that you maintain a high level of service to your clients. You may also want to add additional professional staff who have the ability to do great work and drive revenue to the firm.

Financial Decisions

They say that cash is king. You may want to take a close look at the organization's financial resources so that you're in a position to achieve your business objectives as well as maximize the value of the firm for its partners. This could include the potential sale of the business or cash to carry out strategic decisions. There are both short-term and long-term goals to consider. It's possible short-term goals may occasionally need to be sacrificed to meet longer-term objectives. For example, if you have a large client who has continually beat down your fees to the point that you are at breakeven or just marginally profitable, it might make sense to drop the client and fill that time with higher-margin clients who value your services. In the short term, that may be a tough decision, but in the long term, it can be very meaningful to the firm's profitability and value to part ways. Your firm only has so much capacity. A thin-margin client who absorbs a big chunk of capacity can put a real drag on the overall value of the firm.

Operation Decisions

Operations are the day-to-day creation and delivery of your services. "Operational" refers to the design, planning, and controlling of services you provide to your clients. For example, if you have other personnel, you may decide you need to improve the flow of how services are created and delivered to your clients. What works today may hamper your ability to deliver the same level of services as your operation grows. Personnel space or technology, for instance, can impact the quality of the services you deliver. Finding the optimum balance of service deliverability and the level of expense is a key factor to your profitability.

Summary Of Your Three-Year Vision

Now that you've created a vision for what you want your business to look like three years from now, it's time to bring it all together:

1. I want **Income** of $250,000.

2. I will develop **Revenue** of $625,000 to achieve my income.

3. I will capture the following **clients to achieve my revenue target:**

   a. **Manufacturers** – <u>Seven clients that average $35,000 per client</u> – Each will be a Southern California privately-owned company that has been in business for at least five years, is profitable and is doing between $5 million and $50 million in revenue. The company will specialize in consumer goods or technology products.

   b. **Distributors** – <u>Six clients that average $30,000 per client</u> – Each will be a Southern California privately-owned company that has been in business for at least five years, has between 50 and 150 employees, has operations in multiple states, is profitable and is doing between $5 million and $50 million in revenue.

   c. **Contractors** – <u>Four clients that average $50,000 per client</u> – Each will be a general contractor based in Southern California, who specializes in residential construction for large developers and is doing $10 million to $100 million in revenue. Each will be involved in multi-state projects and have approximately 250 employees or more.

4. I will develop a **Relationship System** consisting of fifteen Level I relationships to help me capture the clients I need.

5. I will do the following **branding activities to strengthen my brand**:

    a. Write one article each quarter.

    b. Give two speeches to CPA firms.

    c. Create content on LinkedIn, Facebook, and Twitter each week.

    d. Do an email broadcast monthly.

6. Strategic, Financial, Operational, Personnel considerations – N/A as I am part of a larger organization

Look at the summary above! Talk about having a plan that maps out the success *you* want! Does it leave any question as to what you'd like to achieve by the end of year three. Is there any doubt as to how you'll make your business vision a reality? Do you have complete clarity on the type of clients you'll focus on and acquire? Are you clear about how you will build your relationship system in order to meet those objectives? Can you see and feel the strength of your brand three years out? You can do this! **It is very empowering to see a picture in your head of the business you want. It's even more exciting to be able to see how you will accomplish it.**

Developing Your One-Year Plan

You've done the hard work. Creating a vision for the business you want takes some thought, but, now that it's done, you can carve out what you'd like to accomplish in the first year. This amounts to simply looking at the three-year plan and deciding how much to chew off in the first year. You assumed that you made $125,000 this past year and in the first year of your plan you decide you would like to earn $175,000. Your plan might look something like this:

Your One-Year Plan
00/00/0000 to 00/00/0000

1. I will make **$175,000 in Income.**

2. I will generate **Revenue of $440,000** to achieve my desired income.

   a. I will need to generate **additional revenue of $160,000** to hit my target revenue.

3. I will capture the following clients needed to achieve revenue:

   a. **Manufacturers** – I will <u>capture two clients that average $35,000 per client</u> – Each is a Southern California privately-owned company that has been in business for at least five years, is profitable, and earns between $5 million and $50 million in annual revenue. Each company specializes in consumer goods or technology products.

   b. **Distributors** – I will <u>capture two clients that average $30,000 per client</u> – Each is a Southern California privately-owned company that has been in business for at least five years, has 50-150 employees, has operations in multiple states, is profitable, and is doing between $5 million and $50 million in revenue.

   c. **Contractors** – I will <u>capture one client that averages $50,000 per client</u> – Each will be a general contractor who is based in Southern California, specializes in residential construction for large developers, and is doing $10 million to $100 million in revenue. Each is involved in multi-state projects and has approximately 250 employees or more.

4. I will add to my PRS by developing <u>five Level I relationships.</u>

   a. I will review <u>fifty Level II candidates</u> to ensure hitting my Level I objectives.

5. I will perform the following branding activities to strengthen my brand:

   a. Write <u>one article each quarter.</u>

   b. Give <u>two speeches to CPA firms.</u>

   c. Create <u>weekly content</u> on LinkedIn, Facebook, and Twitter.

   d. <u>Send out a monthly informative email broadcast.</u> By the end of the year, it will be going to 200 people.

6. Strategic, Financial, Operational, Personnel considerations – N/A

Wow! Now you have a great roadmap for getting the results you want over the next year. You have complete clarity on the clients you will go after, and how many you will need to meet your revenue goal. Because *you* are clear about what these clients look like, as you build your relationship system, your Level II candidates and Level I relationships will have a very clear picture of the type of clients you work with. Make no mistake: This clarity will help strengthen your brand, which eventually will create a very strong mindshare position.

In the revenue section, we discuss total revenue needed to achieve the income goals that you have. Some professionals do transactional work, which involves one-time projects for clients who don't repeat. Other professionals do work that is recurring. That is, they have clients who require similar services each year.

In this example, as an insurance broker, you renew the coverage each year for the client. On average, an insurance broker can count on about 90% retention of his or her "book of business" renewing. A recurring business is attractive, because you build a foundation of revenue and achieve your annual goals by assuming 90% retention of your current business (which assumes you provide great service to your clients), plus the generation of the additional revenue you will need to achieve your goal.

For our illustration, we calculated that you would need $440,000 in revenue to make $175,000 in personal income based on your 40% split. Since you made $125,000 the year before on revenue of $313,000, and are assuming a 90% retention rate, that means that you'll need to produce a total of $160,000 of new business in order to achieve your goal of $440,000 in total revenue.

You'll also note that the first-year plan includes the development of five new Level I relationships and a review of fifty

Level II candidates. Remember that it takes eight to ten Level II candidates for every Level I that you develop. You are looking for a very special person and relationship, and most people will not be able to make it through the "*ripening tomato process*" without being deleted from your relationship system.

I know you're thinking that five new Level I relationships are no big deal, but I can assure you that, if you're doing things properly, getting to five Level I's is a major accomplishment. Developing five new Level I relationships over the course of a year is challenging because it takes a lot of focus and managing your system properly. But it is worth it!

The good news is that for every Level I you develop, you have just made your business a little bit more predictable and valuable. You will be in the number one mindshare position with people who will deliver for you. It also means you are depending less on random referrals to achieve your goals.

Developing Your First 90-Day Plan

Now that you've laid out what you would like to accomplish over the next year, you need to tactically understand how to make that happen. The first step is to break out what you would like to accomplish in the first ninety days. Once you have that established, you can then break out what you'll do in the first thirty days to achieve your "90-Day Plan."

Your plan might look like this:

90-Day Plan
00/00/0000 to 00/00/0000

Clients:

1. **Manufacturers** - Identify <u>ten</u> suspects and develop <u>two</u> potential prospects.

2. **Distributors** - Identify <u>ten</u> suspects and develop <u>two</u> potential prospects.

3. **Contractors** - Identify <u>ten</u> suspects and develop <u>one</u> potential prospect.

Relationship System:

1. <u>Go through my contact management system and identify any possible Level II candidates</u> and add them to my relationship system.

2. <u>Add ten new Level II candidates.</u>

3. Develop <u>one new Level I</u> relationship.

Branding:

1. Write <u>one article</u> each quarter.

2. <u>Identify one CPA firm</u> whose partners can benefit from my talk on risk analysis.

3. <u>Set up an initial distribution list</u> and <u>send out three informative monthly email broadcasts.</u>

4. <u>Add ten names to my email distribution list.</u>

As the "90-Day Plan" illustrates, it's important to identify very specific tasks that you will do to move your business forward. Once you break things down, you'll see just how clear and doable it all is! Plus, none of it will interfere with your ability to do your work.

The last step is to break out your first "30-Day Plan." The approach is to carve out how much you want to do in the first thirty days of your "90-Day Plan." It could look something like this:

First 30-Day Plan
00/00/0000 to 00/00/0000

Clients:

1. **Manufacturers** - <u>Identify ten suspects</u> and connect with them.

2. **Distributors** - <u>Identify ten suspects</u> and connect with them.

3. **Contractors** - <u>Identify ten suspects</u> and connect with them.

Relationship System:

1. <u>Go through my contact management system and identify any possible Level II candidates</u> and add them to my relationship system.

2. <u>Add three new Level II candidates.</u>

Branding:

1. <u>Identify a topic</u> for an article.

2. <u>Set up an initial distribution list</u> for my email broadcast.

3. <u>Send out one informative monthly email broadcasts.</u>

4. <u>Add 3 names to my email distribution list.</u>

Voila! There you have it: Very specific tasks that will not interfere with your ability to do work for your clients and that will definitely move your business forward. At this point in your career, it's not going to be big things that make a huge difference for your business—it's going to be the little things that really have an impact.

When you did your three-year vision of what you wanted the business to look like, I'm sure it felt a little overwhelming. But when you broke out the first year, you probably began to think that it might be doable. When you then created the first "90-Day Plan" and then finally what you were going to do in the first thirty days, I'll bet you looked at it and said, "I can do this!"

Once you develop your three-year plan, one-year plan, "90-Day Plan," and have identified what you'll do in your "30-Day Plan," put the other plans aside and keep the "30-Day Plan" in front of you. Upon completing your first "90-Day Plan," you simply go back to your annual plan and extract what you want to do in the second 90-day period. Then, you extract what you want to do in the first thirty days of that second "90-Day Plan," just like you did here in this example. **I cannot overemphasize the importance of keeping your "30-Day Plan" in front of you.**

In fact, I suggest to my coaching clients that they keep a copy of their "30-Day Plan" on their desk, in their car, and even on their bathroom mirror. Again, keep it in front of you, so the steps are top of mind and you get them done. When you start checking the tasks off and *see* you're making progress, you'll feel confident and empowered. You'll feel . . . in control. Know why? Because you *are*. "Out there" is no longer controlling you.

I want to offer one last important note. I suggest that you revisit your three-year vision at the end of each year and make any adjustments you feel are appropriate. Then, when you extract the annual plan, you will be doing it with an up-to-date vision of where you want to take your business.

Okay, now that you have a vision for where you want to take your business and, more importantly, how you can get there, I'm sure you're excited to get going, right? Whoa! Not so fast.

Remember back in Chapter 2 when we talked about what comprises your brand? We said that your brand is 20% utility and 80% perception. **With this chapter, we've just finished clarifying your utility by developing a vision and a plan.** Now comes the *really* important stuff—the remaining 80%—that has to do with you and how you are perceived. In the next chapter, you'll create the vision and plan for a satisfying personal life that will contribute to the strength of your brand.

8

PERSONAL GOALS
Keep You On The Front Burner

"There's nobody who cares more about you than you, and there's nobody better equipped to take care of you than you."
—*RUSH LIMBAUGH*

How we come across to others can make or break our ability to gain mindshare. All things being equal in terms of technical skills, if an individual decides to work with you, it's because of some "likeability factor" you have—such as the energy you display or the way you light up when you talk about your kids—that gets them to react with "This person's the right choice for me." Consciously or not, we're always influencing some people in a positive way and others in a negative way. **We have no control over someone else's perception and what makes them do what they do or think what they think. But we can influence how they feel when they are with us.**

However, I think it is fair to say it starts with how we feel about and take care of ourselves. Over the years, I have seen many dedicated professionals pour their hearts out for their clients while virtually ignoring their personal lives. If they were people who worked with me, I implored them to take themselves off the back burner and put themselves on the front burner. Ironically, many of them didn't see that not taking care of themselves personally would hurt them professionally. How? Your clients will be negatively impacted if your personal life goes upside down. Your troubles will also influence the behavior of people who have the ability to refer clients to you. If they perceive there is something negative going on in your personal life, they will pass on you and give their referral to the next person (your competitor), who they perceive to be in sound physical and mental health. Remember: Anyone who refers you wants to look good in the eyes of that client. Their reputation is at stake, and they won't risk your tarnishing it.

In the last chapter, you created a vision for the business that you would like to see over the next three years. **It is equally important to have a vision of where you would like to have your personal life be in that same time frame.** For the purposes of creating that vision, we have typically focused on six specific areas: health, spouse and family, finances, hobbies, spirituality, and education. Let's create that personal vision together.

Your Health

Good health is vital to your professional life. If your health goes, nothing else matters. Have you ever had a bad case of the flu, where you're lying in bed, achy and miserable? Were you thinking about the office or issues that you needed to address at work? I'm guessing no. If you're like me when you're in that state, you're just feeling really lousy and not thinking about anything other than getting better. When we're feeling good, we have a tendency to take our health for granted. Our bodies are the machines that make everything else go. If that machine breaks down, it affects our entire lives.

A couple of years ago, when I was starting with a new coaching client, we got to the health section of his plan—and he immediately told me he didn't have time to exercise. This client, who we'll call "Jake," said he had young kids, so it was too difficult to exercise in the morning, and evenings didn't work because he and his wife were likewise busy doing homework with the kids and tending to other family activities.

Jake knew he was overweight and out of shape. In both of our two previous meetings, he appeared tired and sluggish. When he said he simply couldn't afford the time to exercise, I promptly responded he couldn't afford *not* to carve out some time to take care of himself! This was a classic case of someone putting himself on the back burner because nobody hassled him about *him*. I told Jake that *we* needed to put him on the front burner—and that, for the sake of himself, his family, and his clients, the front burner was where he needed to be all the time. He would let everybody down if he suffered a serious health issue that could've been avoided by taking better care of himself.

After some cajoling, I got Jake to agree that it was important for him to make some lifestyle changes and improve his health. By the third year, his vision was that he would be exercising four days a week, have lost 50 pounds, be eating healthy, and have his body fat down to less than 20%. He committed to working out three days a week during the time he would usually have lunch. He joined a local fitness center and worked out during a time that would not impact his family. I literally watched an individual change his life in so many ways by committing to get healthier. By just starting to realize his three-year vision for his health, Jake felt better about himself. He became noticeably more energetic and enthusiastic. He also became much more confident in who he was and what he could accomplish.

We are walking billboards for our services. It is important that we have the energy and vitality to attract the clients we want. Our "package" must be compelling to others for them to be excited to work with us and to refer clients to us. How we present ourselves is an important part of our brand and our ability to gain strong mindshare with another professional. As an example, if someone is looking to refer a litigator for a client, they want someone dynamic who will fight for them. If a litigator they know is clearly out of shape and comes across as lethargic, there is little chance that person will get the call. Please don't misunderstand me! **We are not talking about being bodybuilders or models. We are specifically talking about having energy and presenting ourselves in a professional way.**

So, imagine that we are here three years from today and you are in great shape and feeling good. What will you have done to get there?" Perhaps your goals would look something like this:

1. I will exercise four 4 days per week for one hour.

2. I will weigh 190 pounds.

3. My body fat will not exceed 20%.

4. I will eat healthy.

5. I will monitor my cholesterol level so that it does not exceed 200.

Were you able to come up with some healthy goals based on this example? I hope so. Health is very important as it impacts everything that we talk about in this book.

Your Spouse and Family

If you are married (or planning to be one day), know this: **Your spouse is your number one partner, and, therefore, deserves**

the appropriate attention in your life. If you're like most, your life as a service professional is extremely busy. We all have a tendency to take those closest to us for granted, because we believe they will always be there, have our backs, and understand whatever we do unconditionally.

Nothing could be further from the truth.

Unfortunately, this attitude is often the precursor to divorce. Think about it. Why would anyone want to be with someone who takes him or her for granted, especially when they should be treating him or her as special?

Have you ever known anyone going through a divorce? Divorce turns your whole life upside down—and people can see it. It can take years to get over such a devastating situation, especially if you have children. The guilt one feels can put a person in a different, painful mindset that can only be healed with the passage of time. You might think you can hide the upset, but you can't. Even people who have known you for quite some time will be reluctant to give you any referrals, because quietly they are saying to themselves, "Something is going on with so-and-so and he/she is not in a good place mentally. I think it would be better if I called someone else."

Your spouse and how they feel is as important as any client you have. By the way, I'm not pontificating here; it happened to me as well. Even though mine was an amicable divorce, it still impacted me for quite some time.

When I started ProGrowth, I decided to make sure that this section "Your Spouse and Family" was part of everyone's plan so that they might avoid going through what I did. Because of what I learned 25 years ago, I enjoy a great relationship with my second wife. **We are partners in every sense of the word.**

To show appreciation to their spouses, I ask clients to plan (there's a key word!) different things, such as one-on-one time nightly, a date night once a week, a three-day weekend once a quarter, flowers once a week, a special vacation once a year, or some other action which is important to them. Regular "spouse time" keeps the proper focus and helps you feel good about your relationship. It's the type of happiness that definitely comes across to others and helps your brand.

Being a service professional is not easy on the family. The need to spend many hours away from home and the kids is always stressful for the professional. The time away creates a constant internal battle between work and family. It can set the stage for a lot of guilty feelings, which tend to play tricks on your mind. The associated stress can build over time and affect the way you come across to others.

The solution is to come up with ways that will allow you to stay connected to your family, and to feel good about the work you are doing on their behalf. Start by identifying specific actions to fuel a family-oriented plan. For example, these might include one-on-one time with each of the kids each month, family dinners so many times per week, family vacations, and other activities and events with extended family. Making family time a priority can give you a high sense of purpose in your professional life. It is a much better feeling when you leave the house each morning knowing that you are connected to your family, the people who are front and center in your life. **Somehow, this is the connection that makes everything else seem worthwhile.** And, believe me, when you're feeling good about the personal part of your life, it comes through in the way you present yourself and communicate in your professional life.

Your Financial Situation

Have you ever met anybody you knew was living beyond his or her means, but wanted to keep up a certain image? Unfortunately, I have. These people have no wiggle room and are totally focused on getting the next client or handling the next case so they can keep the revenue and income coming. Their stress is self-evident, and easy to pick up on, because people in this position rarely take an interest in others. They are more concerned about what other people can give them than how they can work together.

When you don't have your financial house in order, things can get tense. Financial stress can affect both your home and your professional life in many different ways. It can be consuming and put incredible pressure on your family dynamics and on the next business deal. Again, you might think you can hide your distress, but people sense it. They'll never say anything, but in all likelihood your chance of getting a solid mindshare position is minimal.

In thinking about your goals, you might want to consider some of the foundational financial objectives that will give you peace of mind and ensure that you and your family are on the path to enjoying the fruits of your work. Some ideas may include: no short-term debt, buying a new home, saving for the kids' education, or maxing out your retirement savings. It's inspiring to know where your income is going to come from, and how your hard work will help you meet your longer term financial objectives. Knowing where you are going and being on a solid financial path gives you that little extra energy when you are with other professionals. It has a positive perceptual impact on your brand, which, in turn, helps you develop strong mindshare.

Taking Time for a Hobby

Your life as a service professional is always about serving others. The responsibilities that come with that can be overwhelming. Do you take downtime just for yourself? Do you have something that you really enjoy doing that channels your energy in a different direction? Having a hobby can be a great way to get away from it all and be absorbed in something that gives you enjoyment. It is a relaxing time that is reserved for you. It's a way for you to recharge your batteries. Sometimes just sitting around feels good, but having a hobby can be even better, since it's "free time" that allows you to feel productive.

A hobby can also be a great social outlet. Playing golf, being part of a book club, doing photography or antique collecting, or being a member of a tennis club are just a few ways you can enjoy a hobby and also connect with others on a social level. As service professionals, we spend most of our time with people who are in "work" mode. These encounters require us to be "on" all the time—to observe certain rules of decorum. Sometimes, it just feels good to let our hair down and be ourselves with people we really enjoy on a social level.

I have always included hobbies in the plans of ProGrowth members for the reasons stated above and to reduce the impact of chronic stress. There is no doubt that being a service professional is very gratifying, yet very stressful. One of my clients, a highly regarded bankruptcy lawyer, thoroughly enjoys his work, but knew that he had to get away from it from time to time because of the demands of the profession. As a hobby, he and his wife take three to four cruises every year to different places. They get the best suite on the ship available and really enjoy themselves for ten days. One of their favorite things to do is to sit on their balcony reading a favorite book. Not only is the time on the cruise a sanity saver, but looking forward to it is equally important. When this client is in the middle of a highly stressful and incredibly complex commercial bankruptcy, he can pace himself to do his best work, because he knows the next cruise is around the corner.

So, having the hobby of "cruising" really does two things for this client... First, the time away completely recharges his battery, because he is enjoying relaxing with his wife, along with the social aspects of cruising. Second, when he is working, he is able to deal with the pressures associated with his work, because he has something he really looks forward to. Being able to keep the stress under wraps gives him the ability to communicate with other professionals in a calm, professional manner. There is no question that this helps strengthen his brand and in turn helps to create strong mindshare with others.

Your Spirituality

Everyone defines spirituality in terms of what it means to them. Some people associate spirituality strictly with religious beliefs, while others associate it with nature, art, meditation, or inner peace/harmony. The question is, "Do people who have spiritual beliefs have an advantage over those who don't?

There is a growing body of research that suggests spirituality does help some people to deal with stress and remain calm in challenging situations. It's not about the higher purpose curing illness, but rather the strength and discipline the belief gives the person that enables them to maintain a healthy balance in life.

Through the years, I have had many clients whose spirituality was as important as anything in their plan. It was the rock that gave them the strength to do everything else. One of those clients was an attorney who had a very supportive wife and six boys. He had a very successful law practice and was highly regarded in his firm. Now, you can imagine having a large family and a successful law practice might require more time than is available on any given day, right? Not for this man. He was Jewish and very devoted to his faith. Each morning, he got up extra early so that he could study the Torah for a half-hour before he started his daily workout. During the year, there were numerous times his faith required him to either leave work early or to not work for a full day or more. For some people, this would create incredible stress and cause them to sidestep their faith with the excuse that they had to "get it done." Not this individual. He always told me that his faith gave him the strength to handle everything else. So, adherence to it took precedence in his life.

There are many other examples of sacrifices this client made during the years we worked together that I could share with you. Some would make you shake your head in disbelief. Not once in the years that we worked together did I ever know him to be anxious. He was able to compartmentalize everything and keep things in proper perspective.

I have been privileged to work with many professionals of various faiths. No matter the religion, the common thread, for some, was that their faith was front and center. The sacrifices I witnessed were amazing. As an example, one of my accountants, after a very long day, would visit the sick and the elderly from his church until late in the evening a few days a week. For him, the visits were meaningful and gave him purpose.

I have also had many clients who practiced mindfulness. Whether it is taking ten to twenty minutes a day to meditate or do yoga, these activities often help people clear their minds and be in the moment. Because service professionals live such busy lives and are constantly multitasking, they can find it very easy to lose awareness of the present as they attempt to juggle everything in their professional and personal lives. Worse, this lack of presence can hurt both personal and professional relationships. You may not realize it, but when you're overloaded, people pick up on it. They can tell that, though you may be sitting across from them at a table or speaking to them on the phone, you're not really "there," and are just going through the motions of being present. Chances are, they'll try to cut short any conversation you're having, and walk away with a bad impression of you.

Have you ever found yourself eating a meal while watching TV or working, only to look down at an empty plate and wonder where all your food went? Or driven somewhere, arrived at your destination, and realized you don't remember much of the trip? If so, welcome to the human race! Our lives are on overload, and it's very easy to miss the important parts of it. I will never forget during the early part of my career when an Irish bartender (who was a great old gentlemen) at a golf club I belonged to said, "Ken, you need to stop rushing through life and start smelling the roses." I used to get to the club about ten minutes before my tee time, hurry in, change clothes, and then run to the first tee. Finally, after watching me do this for quite some time, my bartender friend felt compelled to give me that great advice. I became much more conscious of what was going on in my life, and have since learned, for the most part, to appreciate staying in the present as much as I can.

At first, some of my clients who saw "spirituality" on the plan template were wondering why I would include this section in their plan. You too probably have similar questions. My hope is that I have been able to persuade you that spirituality is an anchor that helps all of us stay grounded—whether it is based in religion or centered on living in the present. As service professionals, we are human beings, not widgets. We are asked to juggle many balls, and are continually examining things we've done so we can learn from mistakes and provide better service to our clients. It's important to be aware that preoccupation with work can cause us not to be "checked in" to our own lives—which can prove damaging. Having an anchor helps us become more aware of our thoughts, feelings, and sensations—and helps keep things steady. When we meet with others, they will be able to see and feel calmness in our demeanor. They will appreciate our ability to be fully present with them. From a business perspective, these qualities will help strengthen your brand, which will help put you in a strong mindshare position.

Your Education and Learning

Stephen Covey had it right in his book, *Seven Habits of Highly Effective People.*: It's important to keep sharpening the saw. In other words, to always be refreshing and expanding your knowledge. One of those saw-sharpening dimensions is education. Covey says, *"Education—continuing education, continually honing and expanding the mind—is vital mental renewal."* We, as service professionals, need to be relevant.

It's not just about staying up with continuing education in your discipline; it's also about learning new things. Once you stop learning, you stop growing. People like to be with people who are interesting and have varied interests.

Some of my clients over the years wanted to learn to speak a language. Others wanted to learn how to play a musical instrument or learn to paint. Some of my clients who weren't proficient using technology wanted to take courses to become more tech savvy, so they could better utilize computers and electronic devices. What about you? As part of your three-year vision, is there something you'd like to learn that would be personally rewarding and give you an added dimension? If so, I want to encourage you to pursue it. You will find that "sharpening the saw" offers a great diversion from the pressures of your work. It will stimulate you and give you a stronger sense of determination. These are all good characteristics to help strengthen your brand and ultimately build strong mindshare.

Summary

I'm hoping by now you're convinced that moving yourself from the back to the front burner—and staying there—needs to be a priority. We cannot bifurcate our professional and personal lives. To feel good professionally, we must feel good personally, and vice versa. If you're a person who has been totally dedicated to your clients at the expense of your personal life, I would like you to give serious thought to what we've discussed in this chapter. I am confident, based on my deep experience working with professionals just like you, that if you change your perspective to one that's more self aware, you'll not only do yourself and your family a favor, but your clients as well. Your loved ones will feel happier and more appreciated, and your clients will get the opportunity to work with you for many years ahead—without your health and personal life imploding.

When it comes to your brand, a healthier, happier you translates into many more opportunities to create the mindshare you want. Simply put, people want to do business with people they perceive to be calm, happy, and in charge of their lives. Project these attributes, and they'll feel good about you and the way you'll represent them if they send a referral your way. Again, you can't control others' perception of you, but you certainly can influence it in a very large way.

The following will help you create a specific vision of how you'd like your personal life to be three years out. Start with a "clean slate," not allowing any past barriers to limit your plans. Once you have identified the goals for where you want to be at the end of Year 3, let it sit for a few days, then come back and make any adjustments. Giving your goals time to sink in will help ensure you got them right.

My Personal Goals
00/00/0000

1. Health

a. _____

b. _____

c. _____

d. _____

e. _____

2. Spouse and Family

a. _____

b. _____

c. _____

    d. _____

    e. _____

3. Hobbies

    a. _____

    b. _____

    c. _____

    d. _____

    e. _____

4. Financial

    a. _____

    b. _____

    c. _____

    d. _____

    e. _____

5. Spirituality

    a. _____

    b. _____

    c. _____

d. _____

e. _____

6. **Education**

a. _____

b. _____

c. _____

d. _____

e. _____

Once you have created your three-year vision, you'll be ready to break it down into what you will accomplish in the first year. As you did with your professional goals, you will then be able to break that down into specific action items for the first year, the first ninety days, and, finally, the first thirty days.

Now that you have a solid foundation for building an attractive brand, it's time to learn how to create the mindshare you want. This is where we really harness your ability to make things happen for your business—and get the referrals you want by making your competition irrelevant.

PART THREE

Creating Strong Mindshare

We now look at what it takes to actually influence and strengthen mindshare. Specifically, we will discuss what you can do or project that will help you win over the mind of a professional who can refer you business, so that they will call you instead of your competition.

In the next three chapters, we will delve deeper into authenticity (being the real you) and its rewards. We will also consider how confidence drives success and why trust is the essential "X Factor" for making anything and everything good happen for your business.

9

AUTHENTICITY
Being The Real You (And Its Rewards)

"Best keep yourself clean and bright;
you are in the window through which you see the world."
— *GEORGE BERNARD SHAW*

Do you have a relationship with another service professional who you like and enjoy being around and who obviously loves the work they do for their clients? My bet is that same professional has a strong mindshare position with you and gets your referrals.

So . . . why is that? In many ways, this person's "hold" over you stems from the fact that they are comfortable with who they are as you are with them, both of you having clarity of purpose. **They are who they claim to be; they are authentic.**

There are many elements that go into being authentic. Brené Brown, the author of *The Gifts Of Imperfection: Let Go Of Who You Think You're Supposed To Be And Embrace Who You Are* said it best when she wrote, *"Authenticity is a collection of choices that we have to make every day. It's about the choice to show up and be real. The choice to be honest. The choice to let our true selves be seen."*

What Is Your True Purpose?

Most service professionals decided on their career choice because they enjoy making a difference for others. Whether you are a consultant, attorney, accountant, investment banker, commercial real estate broker, or other type of service provider, your purpose is to be of service to others by helping them solve their problems or achieve their dreams. That is what gets you out of bed in the morning and why you do what you do. Or, is it?

The altruistic part of me always wants to believe that every professional I meet wants to do what is in the best interest of his or her client. Unfortunately, this isn't always the case. I'm sure you have met people who clearly are in survival mode when it comes to their work. Their sole purpose for doing what they do is to make money to keep the wolves at bay. They are totally self-focused and self-absorbed in finding a client who will be their next payday. Because they do not have any meaningful relationships, they are like scavengers looking for that referral that nobody else wants. Their purpose is not about the client; it is all about money. You will see them at every networking event in town, because they feel a need to keep the machine going. They look forward to meeting new people, because those people don't know them yet and aren't on to their game. We've all heard the stories about these people. They pad their bills, provide unnecessary services, and the quality of their work is typically poor. Their personal lives are a mess. They have very weak brands and almost no chance for mindshare. As a matter of fact, they probably have what I would call "negative mindshare," because there is no chance that they'll be given a referral from someone who really knows them. These are the least authentic people out there.

There are still others, who have a reputation for "doing deals" or churning for commissions or billable hours. The focus is on them and their needs. While they may do good work, if you have an opportunity to refer them, you probably won't, for fear they won't do what's in the best interest of your client. Understandably, if you're aware of another person in the same discipline who is client focused, that person will probably get the referral instead.

Why You Do What You Do

Almost 100% of the time, it is not *what* you do that gets people to work with you and feel comfortable referring clients to you. In his book, *Start with Why*, Simon Sinek suggests that **people's desire to work with you starts with clarity of why you do what you do.** Your profession involves providing specific services to individuals or organizations. You have made a significant investment in your education and experience to acquire the skills necessary to provide value for your clients. Why did you choose to be in your profession? Is it because you enjoy working with people and solving their issues, or is it simply a means to making money?

Sinek believes that you must know and be able to articulate why you do what you do because, ultimately, that "why" is precisely the reason people will want to work with you. **If you do not understand your "why" and can't clearly articulate your purpose, then you will come across as inauthentic, and the relationship will go nowhere.** You've reduced yourself to a commodity. Sinek proposes that to inspire others, start with "clarity of why."

If you're like most service professionals, when you meet someone who has the potential to send you referrals, you start off the conversation by telling them what you do. For example, if you're a lawyer, you might say, "I'm an M & A lawyer and typically work with middle market businesses on issues surrounding business sales." The problem is that most people have heard the same or similar description from many other attorneys, and still have little to no understanding of what they—and now you—do!

Sinek describes "the golden circle," an illustration of a specific messaging approach, as having three concentric rings. The inner most ring is the "why." The next ring out is the "how," and the outer most ring is the "what." The circle concepts are all interrelated and must be in balance. The idea behind the golden circle is that you need to connect with your clients emotionally first, through your "why" story. You then share "how" and "what" you do, which support and authenticate "why."

Sinek believes that you can have *short-term* success by focusing on the "what." If you want to spend your time networking and hoping for the best, then focus on the "what." **But, if you want to build a strong relationship system where you are in the top mindshare position and enjoy a successful long term practice/ business, then you must start with "why," and everything you do must reflect your "why."** Your authenticity is about actions.

Let's go back to our M &A attorney, who, this time, is purposeful and very clear on why he is in his chosen profession:

The "Why"
(Your Heartfelt Story that Inspires People and Communicates Your Authenticity)

"I became an M&A attorney because I believe that owners of businesses who have worked hard over the course of their lives to create the value in their businesses get one shot at monetizing that value when they sell their business. They deserve and expect the best legal representation available to help them realize the highest market value at the time of sale, and they have the right to keep the proceeds once the sale is complete without fear of litigation.

The "How"
(Supports Your "Why")

I work with owners of closely held businesses that have at least $2,000,000 of equity in the business. I believe in working closely with my clients so that we make good decisions based on all the facts as we move through the process together to ensure the highest value is achieved and that there are no issues that could cause problems down the road.

The "What"
(Authenticates Your "Why")

To ensure that my client and I are on the same page, I communicate all legal developments, have a clear understanding that all information good or bad is uncovered, provide timely assessments on progress, and make myself available 24/7 for any concerns my client may have."

If this individual presents him or herself to you in a way that is genuine and authentic, you would probably want to try to get them to a Level I relationship. It is clear they are passionate about "why" they do what they do, which makes you confident any clients you refer will be well taken care of and would, as a result, feel appreciative towards you.

Because of the hyper-competitive world we live in and the pressure to bring in business to our firms, it becomes increasingly difficult to be true to your "why." Sadly, passion can be left behind and replaced by the pressure to bring in business. This state can become a slippery slope. Once people know you and start sensing the pressure you're feeling to produce clients, they begin to view you differently. I know you think you can hide the strain, but people who know you well will pick up on it. So, how can you remain true to the "authentic you," who has a purpose, when you're under that kind of pressure?

The people I have worked with who've had many years of success have always put value first. They steadfastly chose to put the needs of their clients first, to do great work for those clients, and to serve those clients to the best of their abilities. And, you know what? That approach always pays off. These clients never worry about making money, because they know the money will come when creating great value for others. In the short term, it may be appealing to put money first, but if you are in it for the long term, standing by your values and what is meaningful to others will have significant positive implications for your brand and your ability to create strong mindshare.

Seeing Yourself As A Salesperson

The realities of the marketplace require that service professionals in all walks of life be able to create and promote their own personal brand. To be successful, as you have discovered in the preceding chapters, you must invest the time that will put you in a position to get the referrals you want.

On the face of it, this might not seem to be a big challenge. To some people, however, doing what's necessary to build their brand and gain mindshare is a major difficulty, because they can't adopt the proper attitude towards self-promotion. They don't believe they should be relegated to being "a shill for the company." **The connotation of being "in sales" does not align with how they view what they do in their profession.** People with this attitude often argue that they did not invest in education and training simply to become a salesperson. Rather, they did it to acquire the knowledge and skills needed to help clients solve their problems or take advantage of opportunities presented to them.

Professionals who don't see themselves as "salespeople," have a mindset that prevents their being comfortable when the topic is new business in both group and one-on-one situations. I can remember from my PNG days being aware that some of the members who were involved with my groups really didn't want to be there. They were going through the motions, but it was almost like they were offended at having to attend a networking meeting. The only reason they were there was that their managing partner told them they were expected to bring new business to the firm.

There is no question this mindset will affect how you are perceived. Nobody will ever question your motives; they simply will discount your intentions. **It really comes down to a choice.** You can choose to feel cheapened because your perception is that you're doing something that is beneath you and approach your marketing and branding efforts in a half-hearted way. Or, in the alternative, you can change your mindset.

We have made the case that you are a business. Your business provides a very specific service that helps individuals and organizations solve a problem or take advantage of an opportunity. Remember, you are no different than a business that manufactures widgets. That business can be the best widget manufacturer in the world, but if it has no distribution system for getting its widgets into the hands of the customer, being "best" doesn't matter.

The perception of your brand means everything to your business. People you put into your relationship system who will eventually become a Level I will do so because you have demonstrated to them that you not only care about them, but that you have a passion for the work a client needs relative to your discipline.

Your head and your heart are aligned. They are both sending the same message. Your intentions are pure.

If this is an issue for you, why not say to yourself right now, *"I am no longer going to view myself as a salesperson. Whenever I get the opportunity, I am going to give others the ability to get a true sense of my brand. That is, my intention will be to convey the passion that I have in helping clients solve issues. I will take that same approach in finding ways to develop a relationship with other professionals, particularly if I would like to have a Level I relationship with them. I am confident that if they experience me and my intentions—get to know the story of my "why"—they will be very comfortable if the opportunity presents itself, to refer me to one of their good clients."*

By changing your mindset, you will take on a completely different persona. You will no longer have that burr under your saddle holding you back. You will be amazed how people's perception of you will change and how your phone will start to ring as other professionals seek you out to collaborate on solving client issues!

I was fortunate to have as my client an individual who was valedictorian of his high school class, went to Harvard for his undergraduate work and is a Harvard Law School graduate. He was obviously a very bright guy, but, I soon learned, always got his answers out of a book. Let's call him "Jeff."

To Jeff, the thought of having to go out to market his services was repulsive. He felt he had earned the right to have people come to him. When reality hit hard in a downturning economy, Jeff had been an attorney for thirteen years, and had no book of business. The good news was he worked for a prestigious law firm where the partners respected his technical acumen. As a result, he'd always been able to keep up his billable hours, which gave him job security. However, Jeff realized that if the volume of work ever dropped, he might be one of the first to be let go. This caused him significant anxiety. When Jeff and I first met, he was excited about developing a plan and creating a relationship system so he could create a stream of business and be viewed as an "esteemed partner." When we got together each month to review his ProGrowth 30-day plan, he was doing pretty well on almost everything except the goals related to his relationship system and branding. Each time, Jeff would insist he simply didn't have time to invest in relationship-building, because he had to make sure he hit his billable hours—his only claim to fame.

But after about a year of working with Jeff and giving him enough rope, he finally said to me, "Okay, okay, I'll do the relationship and branding stuff. How do I start?" This turnaround in attitude was a big deal, and I was happy Jeff got there on his own timing. **The first thing he needed to do, I said, was admit to himself the importance of developing the right relationships and properly positioning his brand in order to get the clients he wanted.** This will require a major change in mindset. It was clear to me Jeff was honestly seeking help and realized that if he worked with me, together, we could make things happen.

I told Jeff the first step was for him to meet with someone and to focus on him or her. Since Jeff had always gotten his answers out of a book, and here there was no manual, the prospect of a one-on-one meeting was daunting. He was very uncomfortable, as he had no idea what to say or do. To keep it simple, and to ease his discomfort, we agreed that Jeff would look the person in the eye and very sincerely ask how he could help him or her. Jeff would keep the conversation about the other person, and learn as much as possible. We agreed that he would find a way to help the individual. It didn't have to be anything major. It could be offering an idea, an introduction to another person, or some other favor. We also agreed that if he continued to be helpful without seeking something in return, eventually the law of reciprocity would take over and that individual would want to do the same for him.

This change represented a milestone for Jeff. But, it was only the beginning. After a period of months, Jeff started to view himself completely differently. Instead of being a technician (a lawyer), he started to see himself as a relationship builder. He began to realize he actually enjoyed meeting with people and helping them. His mind and his heart were now congruent. As a result, people enjoyed meeting with him, and he became the person everyone wanted to know.

I will never forget being introduced to another professional, and suggesting to her that she meet Jeff. She told me she knew of Jeff and would love to connect with him—but that she'd heard he was booked for three months, because everyone was lining up to meet with him for breakfast or lunch! That information was sweet music to my ears. Here was a guy who transformed himself. For Jeff, changing his life came down to two things:

1. He gave himself permission to remake his attitude about getting "out there," meeting with people, and developing his brand.

2. He took the focus off himself and focused instead on helping others.

As his coach, if I would have continually pressured Jeff to build relationships, in essence forcing him to do something he really didn't want to do, this transformation would never have happened. For us to have mind/heart alignment, we must want something for ourselves, and we must do it at our own pace.

Fast-forwarding nine years later, Jeff is now one of the top producers in his firm and serves on its management committee. His billing hours remain strong and most of the hours are from new clients he has acquired through referrals from other highly regarded professionals. He has become that "esteemed partner," and has achieved the success he wanted.

The moral of the story is that we can be anything that we want to be. But, your head and your heart must align. If they don't, no matter how hard you try to hide it, people will sense the disconnect. Your brand and your ability to create mindshare, so that people look forward to referring you their clients, depends on your not only talking the talk, but walking the walk. If you have lost passion for what you do, you might want to think about pausing before moving forward. Consider carefully whether or not you can turn your mindset around. If you can reignite the flame for your work, by all means, power on! But, if you can't summon the will, it may be time to look for something else to do. Let me tell you something. If you're not honest with yourself and continue doing work you don't enjoy, you will continually be disappointed, because you won't get the referrals you want. Your lack of authenticity will trump your half-hearted efforts every time. But, if you enjoy your work and just need an attitude adjustment about "selling," I would recommend this: Think back to your "why." Why did you get into your profession in the first place? What about it made you excited? How have you enjoyed doing it in the past?

If doing great work for a client is what you envisioned, then going out and sharing that vision—enthusiastically!— with others who have the ability to refer their clients to you should not feel much different.

Carl Jung, the highly respected psychiatrist and founder of analytical psychology said:

> *"It all depends on how we look at things, and not on how they are in themselves. The least of things with a meaning is always worth more in life than the greatest of things without it."*

If your head and your heart are aligned, you will have purpose for whatever you do. Your passion will be obvious—probably even contagious—and people will want to be part of your life.

Once your passion comes out, **confidence** becomes very important in attracting others and creating a strong mindshare position. In the next chapter, we take a look at the implications of confidence and what it can do for you.

10

CONFIDENCE
It Determines The Level Of Your Success

"Nothing binds you except your thoughts; nothing limits you except your fear; and nothing controls you except your beliefs."

—*MARIANNE WILLIAMSON*

Our minds are powerful tools that can make or break our efforts to create the lives we want. Over the past twenty years, I have been privileged to meet some very successful professionals. These were people who did not see themselves as followers, but as leaders. While it's possible others doubted these professionals' ability to achieve success, you could tell their belief in themselves never wavered.

Self-confidence is a differentiator. If you have one group of people who are self-confident and another group who are not and give them the same challenges, the self-confident group will win every time. The road to success is not easy, but many would say it is worth it. There are setbacks along the way, and nobody comes through unscathed. There will be many times that we all get thrown off the horse. But the difference between self-confident and self-doubting people is that self-confident people get back up on the horse and embrace the challenge, while self-doubting people stay on the ground and tell themselves they're not good enough to ride. Self-confident people believe they *will* triumph; self-doubting people believe they *can't*. They allow the world to determine their fate, as they remain imprisoned by feelings of inadequacy.

I've had so many people enter the ProGrowth program whose lack of self-confidence was the primary reason they weren't actualizing their potential. Unfortunately, there's nothing I can say or do that will turn that situation around immediately. But what I can do is show these individuals a path we can go down together and where, at some point, they begin to take control of their lives. That point would become their "Aha!" moment that we would then follow up with a series of little steps designed to gradually grow their self-confidence.

Once these individuals started to experience small bits of success, their transformation would begin. Slowly, I would start to see more bounce in their step, an ease to their body language, changes in how they communicated and, most importantly, the beginnings of a more positive attitude. The great thing about self-confidence is that anyone can get it and keep it provided he or she is willing to go out and work for it. Is self-confidence easy to acquire? Absolutely not. Self-doubters usually have conditioned themselves to think they are unworthy or don't have the ability to live the life they see others living. One of my clients, a professional and a woman, came to me wanting to build a book of business. Let's call her "Eileen." After spending some time with Eileen, it was clear that if we were to work together, we'd need to address some personal issues first. As part of my interviewing process, I like to make sure I understand where a new client is in terms of his or her self-confidence. In this case, it was obvious that Eileen's difficult divorce, while four years in the past, was still affecting her and her self-image. When she talked about the divorce, I could feel the hurt that was still there and the grip this life event had on her psyche.

Pre-divorce, Eileen had been living the American dream. She and her husband had very good jobs and a beautiful home with the proverbial white picket fence. Then, seemingly out of the blue, Eileen's husband said he was no longer committed to their marriage—in other words, he wasn't "all in," even though she was. The ensuing divorce crushed Eileen and created this mental jail cell that told her she was "not good enough" to have happiness or success. Eileen lost confidence at work and missed out on becoming a partner. Once a positive individual who enjoyed life, she quickly took on a persona of a depressed individual—someone who almost questioned her very existence.

For the first six months that we worked together, I didn't see much improvement in Eileen. Her psychological state was clearly affecting the way she was going about developing her business and her brand. I elected to use our time together to let her talk through her issues, since this is often an effective way to release emotions and gain clarity. In addition to these sessions, Eileen attended regular sessions with her peer group in our program. The combination of meetings started to have a very positive impact. Eileen's peer group included other professional women who were very supportive, and also shared some difficult life experiences of their own. This was significant for Eileen, because she was able to hear what these other women endured and were able to overcome. It gave her the confidence to start thinking she could put the horrible experience of her divorce behind her and move forward.

After about a year in our program, Eileen began to take on a different persona. She was ready to get on with her life. It was very gratifying to see Eileen go from being someone who felt sad and hopeless to someone who rediscovered an excitement for life. Suddenly, her eyes were open once again to all the opportunities available to her, all the possibilities of what she could accomplish. I think Eileen's story illustrates that sometimes we need to give ourselves the chance to heal and reboot, so we can approach the starting line fresh and revitalized.

So, what is self-confidence? The dictionary defines it as "trust in one's abilities, qualities and judgment." It's about being self-assured without any doubt. Some people have told themselves, either consciously or not, that they can't be successful because they weren't born with self-confidence—that it's just not in their wiring. I'm here to tell you (in an encouraging way!) that that's an excuse. Many times, I've heard the comment, "I just *wish* I had the confidence so-and-so has." Know what? You *can* have that confidence, but not if you keep holding yourself back with a self-defeating attitude and comparisons to "so-and-so." Would you agree this mindset probably isn't helpful to you personally *or* for gaining mindshare?

Having self-confidence isn't about being all-knowing. Rather, it's about having an unfailing belief in yourself. Think about it: If you don't believe in you, is it reasonable to expect that others will? And, by extension, if you had the opportunity to refer an individual who was self-confident versus an individual of equal capabilities who was not, which one would you refer? There's really no contest.

Self-confidence occurs in the mind. If you believe you can have it, you will. If you believe you can't have it, you won't. A critical component of your brand and the favorable impression others have of it is your self-confidence. People want to know you will not buckle under pressure and that you will inspire and deliver for any client they refer to you.

I hope I've made my case about the importance of self-confidence and the impact it has on your brand. Being self-confident can help you significantly in creating the mindshare you want. If I said anything that resonates—or even hit too close to home—don't be concerned! Know that many, many people have issues with self-confidence—some for the same reasons as you! The question is, "Are you ready to do something about it?" If so, all that matters is that you decide this very moment that you're going to move forward. Acquiring confidence is about doing something every day to strengthen it. Self-confidence does not just happen. It is an attribute just like the many other attributes that we talk about in this book. For you to become fully self-confident, you will need to work at it every day. The more you practice, the more your mind will tell you that you *are* self-confident. Gradually, you'll become so comfortable with this mindset that it will just become a natural part of who you are.

At the beginning of this change, be mindful not to give into your fears. The first few times you do anything that's new or foreign, it can be scary. But, once you see that you can get past that hurdle and remain in one piece, you will know you can do it. Remember, you have made a decision to redefine yourself. Redefining takes time.

Let's look at some things that can positively impact your self-confidence:

1. **Your Appearance:** Coming across as healthy and vibrant lets people know how you feel about yourself. In Chapter 8, we looked at the importance of your health. By having

a consistent exercise program, you'll feel good and exude higher energy. Being physically fit has many benefits. It's been proven time and time again that doing regular exercise and having a reasonably healthy diet will help you feel, look, and perform better. Being in good health has a significant impact on your self-worth that is hard to miss. Plus, choosing to make your health a priority gives you the opportunity to "exercise" self-discipline. When you meet your exercise goal every day by getting to the gym, getting a good workout, and then starting (or ending) your day, you can't help but feel great. Don't worry if you're out of shape or have a few extra pounds. Everyone starts somewhere! Just tell yourself, "Today is the first day of the rest of my life!"

2. **Your Dress:** An important part of our presentation to others is the way we dress. The thought we put into our clothing also sends a message to our mind on how we feel about ourselves. While type and style of dress are often dictated by your profession, it's imperative to always dress neatly. This shows respect for others and for yourself. Never wear something that is soiled or fits poorly. Don't shortchange yourself by pulling an "anyway," like wearing something that has a stain you didn't notice right away. An "anyway" is something that you probably shouldn't do, but do anyway, because you perceive you don't have the time or the inclination to change it. In other words, it's a cop-out. Wearing a suit with a small stain on the lapel that you tell yourself is not that noticeable is "anyway" thinking—and a mistake. You can bet people *will* notice

the stain and they'll judge you for it. Why give them reason to question how you might feel about yourself? Why put yourself in a situation that will make you self-conscious? Wearing something that's neat, clean, and appropriate for the situation makes you look *and* feel good. And, that's important.

3. **Your Body Language:** Your body language telegraphs a lot about your self-confidence and self-image. Here are some body language tips for conveying confidence:

   a. **Posture** – When you're with someone (and even when you're not—it's good practice and good for your well-being!), always exhibit proper posture. Sit up or stand up straight. You want to look tall and self-assured. Slouching sends the message that you're low energy, don't really want to be there, or don't take your profession seriously.

   b. **Be Calm** – Take deep breaths, be in the present, and show your engagement by being quick to listen and slow to speak. Fidgety people come across as nervous and not in control.

   c. **Maintain Eye Contact** - Keep your eyes focused on the person in front of you. Avoiding eye contact comes across as being unsure of yourself, disinterested, unable to focus or, worst of all, untrustworthy.

You've probably heard that your thoughts influence your actions. It's entirely true. And that's why it's important to continuously put yourself in a mindset that avoids negative thought and focuses on thinking positively. The very nature of being a service professional will test your faith in yourself—circumstances beyond your control can have you thinking you're not good enough to succeed at what you do. It is essential that you never stop believing in you. **Your confidence isn't based in who you are; it's based in who you *think* you are.** If you allow the world to shape your self-image, then the world will dictate the way you see yourself.

Most people and situations you encounter in life will be positive, and will boost your self-confidence. While it's always good to be receptive to this uplifting energy, take care to dodge its evil twin, which is negative or "downer" energy. Unfortunately, some people allow negative situations to adversely impact their self-image. You can avoid doing the same—and program yourself to be impervious to all negativity—by choosing your thoughts wisely. If you find you're viewing yourself negatively or putting yourself down, make a conscious decision to stop it immediately. Through practice, you can train yourself to make this response your natural reaction. Don't let circumstances dictate your emotions. Stay in control of your feelings and *choose* how you will feel. Choose positivity.

The golfers who earn a spot on the PGA Tour exemplify what I'm talking about. To make it to the PGA Tour is not easy. Most of the players start playing golf at a very young age. They receive instruction from some of the best teaching professionals and, by high school, are competing in tournaments around the United States and the world. There are only 125 spots available on the PGA Tour. Once you earn your card by going through the grueling Tour school, you must place within the top 125 PGA golfers to be able to keep it.

Every player who makes it onto the Tour needs to continue working on the mechanics of their golf swing, as well as the shots they'll be confronted with on the golf course. **But, the most important thing they must learn is the ability to control their mind.** Everyone hits the ball well, and everyone is superbly qualified to be there. See what I'm getting at? Believe it or not, these incredible athletes deal with the same type of issues we do. They encounter similar common mental obstacles that can keep them from realizing their potential. They too deal with performance anxiety, emotional reactions to situations, and distractions that interfere with their ability to be successful.

The reason Jack Nicklaus achieved such phenomenal success was that he had an unshakable confidence in himself and his ability to overcome any obstacle. He was always prepared. He had a game plan and never got down on himself if the results did not match his goal. He just got back up on that horse (to use our metaphor from earlier), and went out the next day and exceeded his expectations. His advice back then still applies today:

"Ask yourself how many shots you would have saved if you always developed a strategy before you hit, always played within your capabilities, never lost your temper, and never got down on yourself."

In his classic best-selling book *ZEN GOLF: Mastering the Mental Game*, Dr. Joseph Parent, a mental game coach who has worked with many top PGA and LPGA tour players, professes the importance of confidence and how to build and sustain it. Dr. Parent knows what he's talking about: he holds the distinction of helping both Vijay Singh and Cristie Kerr reach number one in the world golf rankings for men and women, respectively. He has become a good friend and I have invited him to speak at a number of ProGrowth events and retreats that we do for professional service firms.

The methodology Dr. Parent uses is his **PAR** approach, which stands for **P**reparation, **A**ction, and **R**esponse to results. These are his keys to confidence and peak performance. He has helped many golfers of all levels get amazing results. You can apply the PAR Approach to golf or any other activity, and it will give you the confidence to succeed. Let's take a look at how we can apply Dr. Parent's methods to a real-life situation.

Assume you've been introduced to an individual, let's call her "Laura," who has an outstanding reputation. Laura has a large book of business with clients you are perfectly positioned to help. She's interested in getting to know you better, to see if you're the person she'd like to refer clients to when they have an issue involving your discipline. It's a significant opportunity for you and you're meeting one-on-one tomorrow.

The first leg of the PAR Approach is **P**reparation. **To prepare properly, Dr. Parent says you must have clarity, commitment, and composure.** Clarity is the quality of knowing what you want to accomplish in your meeting. Mentally, you develop a plan, creating a clear vision of what you would like to accomplish and what you will do to make it happen. Having a plan instead of just showing up gives you more confidence to start the engagement. You see it before it happens, because of the vision you created in your mind. Although Dr. Parent suggests that you refrain from focusing on what you want to avoid, he explains that you should take potential obstacles into account. Nothing ever goes just the way you imagine it should. Being aware of what unwanted direction the meeting might go, and mentally preparing for it, will help keep you from reacting like a deer in the headlights if it actually happens. You're not *looking* for obstacles to arise, but you're ready if they do.

Once you have created your plan and strategy with clarity, it's essential to have full *commitment* to your plan. You must pre-accept the full range of possible results, and then clear any second thoughts or doubt before you meet. This will help you to not obsess over the result, but instead to focus on the process that you've planned, and then let things naturally evolve.

Composure is critical to a sense of confidence, whether you're hitting a golf shot or going into a meeting that can have significant positive implications for your business. To even your emotions before going into the meeting, Dr. Parent suggests that you settle and center yourself through breathing to avoid being stressed, uptight, or speedy in your conversation. While you're in the meeting, continue to breathe deep and feel the calmness. This will have a significant impact on your self-confidence and on the way you come across to the other person.

The second step of the **PAR** Approach is **A**ction. You should act from a focused presence. Remember, your intention shapes your behavior. You need to be aware of your intentions and external circumstances that might have an impact on you. Your intention in this meeting with Laura is to see if you can develop a personal relationship with her, because you believe you would like to make her a Level I relationship if you can get her past all the hurdles. Make sure that you trust your *Secrets of Mindshare* training. You deserve to be in the meeting. Entering the meeting with confidence and mindfulness will create a comfortable environment for your discussion. On the other hand, if you try too hard, it will be counterproductive. Express yourself in a clear way and without attaching your conversation or actions to a result. According to Dr. Parent, your ideal state of mind in the meeting (like in golf) would be one that is free of hope and fear, and beyond confusion and doubt. You should listen openly, communicate honestly, and act with integrity. Focusing on Laura and how you can help her is important. But be sure to avoid over-promising and under-delivering at all costs.

The last step of the **PAR** Approach is your **R**esponse to results. If the meeting goes extremely well, you will want to build your confidence by making statements to yourself that the process you used does indeed work. For example, give yourself a little verbal pat on the back by saying aloud, "My preparation paid off. I can meet with anyone and feel comfortable if I prepare well."

Now, what if you had a decent meeting, but it was only partially successful? Are you going to beat yourself up over it? No! Instead, focus on all the aspects of the meeting that went well. Then, take a look at the areas where you think you can improve that will make the next meeting better.

Lastly, what if the meeting was a disaster? Will you mope around feeling sorry for yourself and seek consolation in thinking, "I knew I wouldn't be very good at meeting anyway"? No way. Tell yourself the silver lining is everything you're going to learn from the experience, so you don't make the same mistakes again. Heck, making mistakes is often the only way to get better at something! Dr. Parent suggests that you snuff out the negative emotional energy with some deep breathing. Do not beat yourself up for doing a lousy job. Learn from the experience by visualizing the outcome you would have preferred. What can you do differently in the future in terms of preparation and action? Take a hard look at your level of commitment. Were you present in the interaction with the individual, or was your head going in one hundred different directions? The key in doing this analysis is to notice—in a non-judgmental way—patterns that appeared, and then apply remedies and adjust accordingly so you do better next time.

Being a PGA Tour player is one of the greatest jobs in the world, but it is also one of the toughest, because so much of it is mental. If you are a Tour player with a young family, it can be extremely difficult, especially if your game is off and you start missing the cut week after week—which means you're not bringing home any income. You can imagine how this plays on a golfer's mind—and golf is predominately a mental game at the PGA Tour level. The Tour is not for individuals with a poor self-image or weak self-confidence.

In many ways, as service professionals, we face the same challenges. Our competitive environments make it extremely challenging to continue to get the referrals we want. My hope is that this chapter has given you a better sense of what confidence means to your ability to have a strong brand and to gain the mindshare that you want.

Jim Valvano, the amazing basketball coach of North Carolina State University willed his players into believing they could become national champions. On April 4, 1983, his team advanced to the final game of the NCAA Championships. They were going up against a Houston team that was supremely talented. It was a foregone conclusion that Houston would win; the only question was how badly they would beat North Carolina State. Coach Valvano told his team that evening that they deserved to be there. He asked the team not to focus on the result, but to focus on the process, work together, and never ever give up. The game had a lot of ups and downs, but the North Carolina team members continued to believe in themselves. After a hard-fought battle, North Carolina State made a buzzer beater dunk at the end of the game and won. To this day, that championship game is still considered one of the greatest upsets in college basketball history.

It just goes to show you how powerful our minds can be. If you really want it, you can go out and grab the brass ring. Sure, there will be ups and downs, but that's what life is all about, isn't it? How can we have the ups if we can't learn from the downs? Life is an experience. Experience is about being exposed to many different situations. How you learn from those experiences will determine the level of your "ups" and help temper the "downs." Use that wisdom to keep building your self-confidence. Remember that believing in yourself makes you—and, therefore, your brand—attractive to others. That's what makes self-confidence one of the key secrets to mindshare!

Now you know why authenticity and self-confidence are key pillars for creating a strong mindshare position. But, the *X Factor* that cements your position is <u>trust</u>. Let's take a look at the concept of "trust" in the next chapter and see what role it plays in our ability to solidify mindshare.

11

TRUST
It Is Your X Factor

"Men acquire a particular quality by constantly acting in a particular way."

—*ARISTOTLE*

The "X Factor" is defined as that one variable in a given situation that can have the most significant impact on the outcome. For you to successfully create mindshare, there is no question the integrity of your brand must be strong. Always. For service professionals, trust is your X factor. As we know, you *are* your brand. Since trust has the biggest impact on how your brand is perceived, people must believe they can count on you to always do what is right—even when no one else is looking.

Acquiring trust takes time and effort. You can never ask for it; you have to earn it. Sometimes, you may find it hard to walk the straight line and live up to the standards that reflect your integrity. If you're ever tempted to deviate from what you know in your heart is the path and go the easy but unprincipled route, just remember this: It takes a lot of time and effort to earn trust, but only a split second to lose it.

Having a professional relationship with another individual who puts you in their number one mindshare position is an honor that should never be taken for granted. There are responsibilities that come with mindshare status. While this person likely has many reasons for agreeing to a Level I relationship with you, I can assure you trust was a major component of their decision-making process. Just as it is for you.

The Level I relationship, as we learned in Chapter 5, is a very special collaborative relationship that is based on trust. It's cemented by an agreement to help one another with one significant event over the course of the year. The foundation of that agreement is the mutual trust you have that each of you will perform for the other person. It is not questioned. For both of you to embrace that sense of trust, you must believe the other person has integrity—that they are true to their word and follow through on their promises. **In other words, a Level I relationship *assumes* mutual trustworthiness.**

So, if trust is that vital to the relationship, how do you make sure it is never compromised? Here are three relationship ingredients for ensuring you never turn trust into mistrust.

1. Transparency – Being transparent in a relationship means you do what you say and say what you mean. In your interactions, you want the other person to have complete faith that anything you share is accurate and not embellished. This is particularly important on the front end of a new Level I relationship. If the person you have agreed to help is expecting you to introduce him to many other professionals in their market and market segments, but you don't have many of those connections, make sure you say so. But, you can also promise the person you will make it a point to find those people who may be helpful to him. Because you have been honest and consistent with your other actions, your commitment will be appreciated.

The lesson here? **Always be upfront and communicative.**

Conversely, never conceal information or allow the possibility of any negative surprises. Once your Level I starts saying to him - or herself, "He didn't tell me that," or "That's not what she said she would do," the relationship is heading south. By being transparent, through your communication and your actions, you will avoid those kinds of situations *and* cement your reputation for having a high level of integrity.

2. Keeping Mutual Trust Intact - If you make a commitment to another person—for example, that you will deliver something or make an introduction by a certain date—it is important to keep it. If you don't meet that deadline, are you violating the trust you have with that individual? You are if you don't say anything different before the deadline arrives. If you have put something out there, the other person deserves to trust that you will come through as promised.

However, there are exceptions. Life happens and plans change. Let's say that you have promised to introduce another individual to your Level I prior to your next meeting that could be very helpful to him or her in a specific area. After a number of attempts, you finally reached the person you wanted to introduce to your Level I—only to learn the person is going to be out of town for two weeks. Coincidentally, that two-week period includes the date of your next meeting with your Level I. You do *not* want to go to that meeting without having fulfilled your commitment. To keep mutual trust intact, it is important that you make your Level I aware of the situation and suggest a new date to make the introduction. Your communication might look something like this:

"Hi, Sue! I had promised to introduce you to Beth Smith, who could be helpful in introducing you to the board of the nonprofit organization you'd like to join, prior to our meeting on the 18th. Unfortunately, Beth will be out of town until the 21st. But, she said she would be happy to meet with you on the 24th or the 25th. Will one of those days work for you?"

Sue responds that the 24th will work perfectly and thanks you profusely for setting up the introduction. Is your mutual trust still intact? Absolutely! You did what you said you would do. There are always going to be situations beyond your control that will prevent you from meeting a deadline on something you promised. When those situations occur, it's critical to inform the other person about the hurdle, and then agree on a new date that works for both parties. Mutual trust and meeting your commitments is paramount in your relationships. Make sure you safeguard them, and keep mutual trust intact.

3. Being Open and Candid - Have you ever been in a meeting with someone you know very well and realize you're both tense because something isn't right between the two of you? If you have, you know it's an uncomfortable feeling that makes it difficult for anything positive to take place. Trust begins to fade and distrust takes center stage.

Let's say, for example, that neither of you is happy about where your Level I relationship is going. No one's feeling the commitment and, unfortunately, no one is willing to talk about the deeper issues that are causing the tension in the first place.

Hey, who said relationships are easy? Whenever you have two people involved, each comes with a different set of expectations based on his or her own perceptions. So, it's completely natural to have disagreements from time to time. The question is, how do you handle those disagreements? Burying thoughts and feelings can drain positive energy out of a relationship very quickly. Most people don't want to hide or misrepresent their intentions, but it's easy to fall into these types of patterns if there's not openness to the relationship. Each party needs to feel they can be candid about their thoughts or feelings relative to any issue that is germane to the relationship.

As with any new serious relationship, people who are in a Level I relationship need time to really get to know each other. But remember, this is a relationship that you hopefully will build on for years to come. A good way to avoid adding unnecessary tension or risk further deterioration is to talk about the expectations you both have for the relationship. You may have certain values, vulnerabilities, or fears that could come into play without the other person having any sense of what's bothering you. By having an open and candid conversation about any misunderstandings and clarifying the purpose of the relationship, you can eliminate any bad vibes and increase mutual respect. Have this conversation from time to time, and you're bound to bond and maybe even laugh together more. In fact, candor could be the very thing that really strengthens your Level I relationship.

I know you might be thinking that too much openness can backfire and potentially kill the relationship. While anything is possible, again, my experience suggests "putting it all on the table" is more likely to strengthen the foundation of the relationship, which will allow it to grow and prosper over the years to come. Any relationship where barriers have been put up and candor has been stifled has little chance of surviving over the long term.

This is not a relationship where you can go on autopilot. You both want it to succeed, so why not give it your best shot? It is important that each of you is comfortable in telling the other about any concerns or expectations without judging what has been shared. You should agree that each of you will just *receive* such information and do your best to fulfill any requests.

Help Like You Mean It

Another very important component of building trust is demonstrating you have a sincere interest in helping and supporting the other person. Little things can go a long way in telling your Level I you value the relationship. Things like, "I came across this article and thought it might be helpful to you," or "I shared your name with a couple of people in a group I belong to who may be able to do some business with you. I'll be sure to let you know if there's any interest." What are you demonstrating with these two types of actions? **You're sending the message that you care about the relationship, and that it's important to you.** You have given, and asked for nothing in return. You have shown a willingness to make it about them, not you.

I have had clients who get upset when they do something for one of their Level I relationships and don't immediately see anything in return. They become antsy and stop investing in the relationship. On a rare occasion, they will find that they rushed to judgment in converting an individual to a Level I relationship. But most of the time, it is simply a case of "I did something for you; now, I expect you to do something for me immediately." Is that demonstrating you care? Not really. You have made the relationship all about you instead of focusing on the other individual. The more ways that you demonstrate that you care and are committed to helping the other person, the more likely that person will learn to trust your motives and embrace the law of reciprocity. That is, they will feel a strong desire to do something for you.

The key to gaining trust in this situation is for you to convey in your words and actions that the *relationship* is important. You never want your actions to suggest—or even allow your mind to think!—that you are using the other person as a commodity to get what you want. The more you try different things to help your Level I, the more you'll learn about the individual. But remember: **You're making a long-term investment in a mutually beneficial relationship that can have positive implications for both businesses.** Do not treat the relationship as a sprint. It is a marathon—and it will get stronger over time.

After reading and digesting this, you might be thinking the cost of Level I relationships is too high in terms of time commitment. Additionally, you may be asking yourself, "If I invest all this time and it doesn't work out, will it have cost me other missed opportunities as well?" Yes, choosing to invest time and energy in Level I relationships is risky. But so is anything else that's worthwhile.

The "ripening tomato" vetting process helps us make sure that if we do convert someone to a Level I relationship, it will be productive for both parties. **Your commitment is critical to the success of the relationship.** If you are "all in," you will be able to build the level of trust that will make the relationship work. The alternative is to have lots of acquaintances you meet at various networking functions where there is *no* commitment and a very high likelihood of *no* referrals. On the surface, this alternative is very appealing, because it requires no effort or investment of time other than collecting names and cards. But, I think we both know at this stage that this is a strategy of hope that offers little chance of long-term success.

Don't be Tagged as a User

It's interesting how some people are always distrusted. They have earned the reputation. Rather than accept them, people are always suspicious of their motives. Almost everything the distrusted person does is viewed as another reason to "consider the source." Once you are tagged with this type of reputation, you stand little chance of ever gaining a strong mind share position with anyone.

You want to be the individual who people always speak well of, even when you're not present. You want to be known for keeping your word and for respecting other people's time by being punctual for meetings and following through on commitments. Even if you make a mistake, people are willing to give you the benefit of the doubt, because they believe you are committed to helping them. You never make excuses. You admit your shortcomings, and you do what's necessary to correct iffy situations. You are a person of integrity. And, you have earned people's trust.

Have Empathy for Others

Empathy plays an important role in building and maintaining trust. Empathy is defined as the ability to understand and share the feelings of another. Successful professionals who have mastered the ability to empathize with others understand the importance of putting themselves in someone else's shoes.

You have learned the mechanics of taking someone through the *"ripening tomato"* process and then converting them to a Level I relationship. But, those are the mechanics. Just because you complete the mechanics does not mean the relationship will produce results. After all, you're not dealing with an inanimate object; you're dealing with a human being who has strengths and weaknesses, greatness and frailties—just like you.

To have a successful Level I relationship, you need to take an honest and dedicated interest in the other person and his or her business. **No one can be successful by themselves. We all need others who are willing to work with us and support us in achieving the results we want.** Empathy is about understanding both the emotional and the logical rationale of another individual without being judgmental. Your success depends on your ability to adapt to and build on the strengths of the other person. Those who are simply focused on what they can get out of another person without empathy for their situation will, in the long term, have a difficult time gaining mindshare and, consequently, the type of referrals they want to grow their business.

Know that going into the relationship the other person will not be viewing it through your kaleidoscope. You must be willing to compromise and meet people where they are. Some will catch on immediately, and you'll be excited about the relationship. Others may have potential, but won't grasp the opportunities and responsibilities of a Level I relationship until later. Having empathy for them and the way they look at the world will help you support them, because ultimately they are looking for the same type of success that you are.

As a professional coach, I know that each client I work with comes to me with a different set of circumstances and orientation. They also come with different social styles. Some social styles make it easier to work with people than others. My job is to help clients get the results they want, and I do so by putting myself in their shoes to get a sense of where they are so I can guide them in developing the relationships they desire.

I always take the position that each of us has the ability to become a rainmaker. Rather than force my way of thinking onto my clients, I have always felt if I can give them enough information and support, they will eventually discover the rainmaker within. I'm happy to say I have many examples of clients who never would have thought they could drive business growth, but are definitely rainmakers today! In fact, they have developed the kind of business that has allowed them to achieve a high level of success and to be esteemed partners in their firms.

I must also say that not every client is a success story. I have had individuals who were unwilling to let go of long-held beliefs. It was clear why they weren't successful. The only way a relationship can be successful is by having empathy for the other person and being open to new ideas. Some have a difficult time with that paradigm. They cannot let go of the networking mentality, where people are used and then forgotten. They cannot wrap their minds around the concept of helping someone without a "what's in it for me" attitude.

Empathy is like any other skill that we learn. Is it worth your while to enhance your ability to empathize with others? Absolutely. It will give you the opportunity to better understand the needs of your Level I's and to help them in a positive way.

Having empathy will help you to better understand what other people aren't saying, but are communicating through their body language and energy. Having empathy will help you better comprehend how they view a relationship with a client, and what their expectations would be if they put you in front of one of theirs. Empathy will help you learn how to motivate others so that together you can achieve the success that you both want. Empathy will allow you to expand your own vision and knowledge, because it will expose you to the perspectives of those around you. **Being empathetic actually benefits *you* by enabling you to get new ideas, as well as more efficient and effective ways to grow your business and improve your life.**

An important element of empathy is grasping the effect you have on others in terms of the words you use and the actions you take. It will give you the ability to better predict how your Level I's will react in certain situations.

Overall, the benefits of being empathetic are significant. It's not just "getting" what's going on with other individuals and what they're feeling, but what you can do to have a positive impact on them. The life of a service professional can be very lonely at times. Having the type of relationships where you can empathize with others helps them feel less alone and motivates them to do what they can to make the relationship a success. It's also how you create strong mindshare and make your competition irrelevant.

If you ever deal with hard-core, "black and white" individuals who don't like to express their feelings, be prepared for them to treat you with suspicion at first. My recommendation is to continue to be you and to show concern for them. After they realize you're not being manipulative and that you truly care about them, they will begin to trust you more quickly than they do others.

When you're able to genuinely share in someone else's joy and excitement, or lend a sympathetic ear in times of trouble, you will be very much appreciated. When someone feels heard, he or she is more likely to listen in return and be "all in." So, even if you're dealing with someone who is very reserved, don't give up on them! They may just need a bit of time to loosen up and drop the protective façade they've had on for a long while. Remember, they are still human. Somewhere deep down, they appreciate the empathy that you genuinely show. You will have their respect, and most importantly the X Factor trust, key ingredients for creating a strong mindshare position.

Look at all the ground we've covered: we have learned what mindshare is: how to develop a foundation to make it happen, and how to create it. Next, we turn our attention to keeping mindshare once you have it—because having mindshare is integral to your long-term success.

PART FOUR

Keeping Mindshare Strong

The last leg of our journey together addresses how **you** can **maintain** a strong mindshare position. As you have learned, securing mindshare with someone takes a lot of time and effort. Once you earn it, you want to make sure it's yours for a long time.

In the final three chapters, we address three critical components that serve as mindshare armor. We will be discussing the "3 Invincible C's"—Conviction, Commitment and Consistency—and how they're all powerful at protecting your number one mindshare position. Afterwards, we'll take a close look at what patience and perseverance mean to your long-term health, personally and professionally. Finally, we wrap things up by addressing what it really takes to pull it altogether—the spotlight is on **you**!

12

THE INVINCIBLE C'S
The Armor That Protects Your Mindshare

"Conviction is worthless
unless it is converted into conduct."
—*THOMAS CARLYLE*

As you have learned, identifying a special person and taking them to Level I relationship status is a process. Then, the challenge becomes creating mindshare with that person. Now, we must look at the elements that will make your hard work pay off and keep you in a strong mindshare position for years to come.

Conviction, commitment, and consistency—what I like to call "**The Invincible C's**"—make up the secret sauce of mindshare. When you have all three C's, you have such strong armor around your mindshare position that it is virtually impossible for your competition to poke through, let alone take a stab at your spot. Let's consider each "C" independently and then discuss what happens when you combine them in a formidable defense for your mindshare position.

CONVICTION

Have you ever noticed how thick the concrete is on an interstate highway overpass? I know maybe you haven't, but as someone who lives in California, I'll admit it's crossed my mind a few times. Here in the Golden State, we can have an earthquake at any given moment. I'm always amazed how we don't have more damage! One of the keys to making sure the concrete holds up is the rebar that reinforces it all. While concrete is strong in compression, it's relatively weak in tensional or torsional strength, meaning it will break or crack when bent or twisted. Adding steel to the concrete (rebar) gives the concrete strength so that it can withstand any kind of assault.

Think of <u>conviction</u> as the rebar that gives you the ability to handle anything that comes your way. Have you ever heard someone say, "She has the strength of her convictions"? To achieve the success you want, conviction is a must-have. Without it, you simply won't be able to handle the ups and downs of building a business and the life you desire. Ask yourself, "Do I truly believe in what I am doing?" If you can answer that question affirmatively, without any qualification or hesitation, then you have conviction. Just like rebar, conviction is a necessary reinforcement for staying strong, so you can work through struggles and disappointments. Inevitably as you grow your business and relationship system, there will be setbacks and times when things go wrong. At those moments, when it may seem your whole world is caving in, conviction will see you through. The same way that rebar holds interstate concrete together during a terrible earthquake, your conviction will reinforce and hold you together, so you can go on for another day.

Jeff Bezos and the Birth of Amazon.com

In 2010, Amazon.com founder Jeff Bezos gave the commencement speech at his alma mater, Princeton University. In the speech, Bezos asked the students if they would ultimately be known for their cleverness or for their choices. He wanted them to ponder, "Will you wilt under criticism, or will you follow your convictions?"

The question gave the students some insight into Bezos's own beliefs. When he decided to start Amazon, Bezos had a great job on Wall Street, made a very good income, and had just been married a year. When he asked his wife about pursuing his dream of becoming an inventor by starting a company that would sell books on a thing called the Internet—which, incidentally, was growing at the rate of 2300% per year—she told him to go for it.

But when Bezos shared his plan with his boss, the boss took him for a walk and promptly told him that he thought it was a good idea for someone who didn't have a job—unlike Bezos, who not only had a good job, but a very good income, *and* the potential to do even better. While his boss's comments gave him pause, after thinking about it, Bezos decided to follow his convictions. He told his wife there was a good chance his idea would fail, because it was an experiment, but he was going to give it everything he had.

Bezos left his cushy job that paid a lot of money and started Amazon.com out of his garage with a couple of employees. After testing the software and inviting 300 people he knew to be beta testers, he decided to go forward and officially started the company in July 1995. The rest, as they say, is history. In 1995, the Amazon.com did about $500,000 in revenue. It ended 2013 with revenue exceeding $75 billion.

Once he saw the success that his online bookstore was having, Bezos decided he could duplicate the success in other markets. As of this writing, Amazon.com touches almost every area of our lives. While the revenues are enormous, Wall Street believes the company is just scratching the surface of the markets it's currently attacking and will attack in the future. Bezos continues to stand by his convictions, and keeps putting profits back into Amazon.com for the long term—which is tough for a public company, since Wall Street wants to see profits. Bezos has been steadfast in that strategy and, at least for now, Wall Street must believe in him, because Amazon.com stock is at all-time highs. As Bezos asked Princeton students in his 2010 commencement speech, "When it gets tough, will you give up, or will you be relentless in your convictions?" Obviously, Jeff Bezos is the type to go with the latter.

Having the Ultimate Conviction: Navy SEALs

When it comes to conviction, no one stands stronger than the United States Navy SEAL. Just getting accepted into the SEAL program requires a very special person. The candidate must be able to pass extremely rigorous physical and mental tests. If you're selected for the program, your "reward" is to spend nine months training in a pain-filled environment, where you're put through grueling physical and psychological training. The washout rate is 70% to 80% of the candidates who start. The only possible way to complete that type of training is to have such deep convictions as to why you want to do it, coupled with an amazing belief in your ability to achieve the "impossible."

The Navy SEAL code is an affirmation of a SEAL's conviction, which he lives by every day. ... *"I will never quit. I persevere and thrive on adversity. My nation expects me to be physically harder and mentally stronger than my enemies. If knocked down, I will get back up, every time. I will draw on every remaining ounce of strength to protect my teammates and to accomplish the mission. I am never out of the fight."....*

I am not suggesting that you must have the mental toughness of a Navy SEAL to achieve the success you want. **What *is* important is understanding that if you totally believe in yourself and what you are doing, you can accomplish anything you want.** Our minds are amazing tools and they have the ability to help us go well beyond what we ever thought we could accomplish.

COMMITMENT

<u>Commitment</u> is defined as a promise to do or give something. It is a promise to be loyal to someone or something. Commitment is not about over-promising or under-promising; it is about making sure that your effort is in line with your conviction.

Because of the very busy lives we all lead, we might mean well in terms of the commitment we make to someone, but if we are unable to follow through, it sends a very mixed message. Commitment is about sticking with something. The more committed you are to doing something, the better you get at it. Gary Player, a well-known golfer who's played professionally for four decades, often said, "The more I practice, the luckier I get" when asked how important skills are when hitting various golf shots. Like anything in life, if something is a priority to you, you will commit yourself to doing it.

To get where you are today has been no easy feat. You've had to withstand the rigors of getting an education and, upon its completion, found yourself officially on your own. You and only you have the power to create the life you want. Getting there requires commitment to take it from dream to reality. Or, as Albert Einstein put it, *"Only one who devotes himself to a cause with his whole strength and soul can be a true master. For this reason mastery demands all of a person."*

My take on what he said is that unless you're committed, it's hard for anyone to be as good as they want to be. Why? Commitments are powerful. They put you in a different place mentally. They influence how you think and how you come across to others. Have you ever had a conversation with someone and walked away saying to yourself "That person is really committed"? I know I have. People like that don't use the word "try"—it's not even in their vocabulary. They believe you either do something or you don't; there is no in between. When they take something on, they find a way to get it done. **Because they're Committed (with a capital "C"!), when they run into an obstacle, they *find* a solution.** Quitting is not an option. They never look back. They learn from their mistakes and they keep moving forward.

I have no doubt that you are committed to building and sustaining a great business for you and your family. Why else would you be taking the time to read this book? Because of your commitment, I am equally confident that you are the type of person who will be able to handle the bumps in the road and won't stop when the road gets rough. I also know that you are human. As humans, we question our commitment at times and can be mightily tempted by the desire to quit. Many people will "try" to do something, but typically their commitment is weak because they are not "all in." They *will* stop as soon as the road gets rough and, as a result, they struggle to succeed at anything. Your commitment is strong and *you* will see it through. **You are just as good as the next professional, but one of your differentiators is your deep Commitment to being the best you can be.**

Never commit to anything unless you are willing to give it your best effort. You will always be confronted with opportunities when you're actively seeking to grow your business. The trick is to choose from those opportunities wisely, and to not commit to more than you can handle. As you develop your business plan, you might see a number of market and market segments that are attractive both from a client perspective and from a revenue perspective. It might be tempting to include a number of those to give you more of an opportunity to get referrals. However, if you cannot absolutely commit to every market and market segment that you identify, my advice is to not do it. Scale back! The last thing you want to do is compromise your integrity by having somebody walk away from a conversation with you suspecting that you talk the talk, but don't walk the walk.

By narrowing your focus and being totally committed to fewer markets and market segments, you will come to be regarded as an expert in those areas. Professionals will want to work with you because of your perceived specialization, and all parties will benefit in the process.

Steve Jobs, the iconic co-founder of Apple, took commitment to a whole new level. He was not your typical CEO who was focused on achieving financial and operational goals. He really felt that for Apple to win, it had to make unique products. He became famous for talking about—and designing—not just good products, but "insanely great" products. Was he a good manager? Most would say he was terrible. If he didn't think you had the same drive to develop and build great products that he had, he would rip you apart verbally or just fire you on the spot. You see, Job's commitment was so strong he wasn't satisfied with just good design; he wanted great design. Always. Either you bought in to that commitment, or you left the company.

You might ask, "Why on earth would anybody want to work for Steve Jobs?" The answer is very clear. Jobs had people knocking at the door to work for Apple because his commitment to making innovative products was so strong. While Jobs might force you to get out of your comfort zone, doing so made you a better person, forced you to stretch as a professional, and created more value for you in the organization. Those who were thin-skinned and not "all in" (totally committed) didn't last very long. Jobs was very good at sniffing out employees who were there just to collect a paycheck. That culture continues at Apple today and, as of this writing, Apple remains one of the most inventive companies on the planet.

Just like Steve Jobs, you have the ability to inspire and lead the individuals you bring into your relationship system. Once they become a Level I relationship, you and they are going to learn and stretch. That is, their relationship with you will help them grow and prosper. Because they're human, they're not always going to perform the way you'd like. At times, you'll question their commitment to the relationship. There will be moments when you will think, "This person doesn't get it." And yes, on rare occasion, you'll discover it isn't worth the hassle or effort to make the relationship work. But, before you give up too quickly, remember that anything worth pursuing requires you to get out of your comfort zone. When you took the individual through the "*ripening tomato*" vetting process and determined they would make an excellent Level I relationship, you did so with a clear mind. It's easy to give up, but if you persist, there's a high likelihood the person will come to appreciate who you are and the commitment you have to your mutual success.

CONSISTENCY

Having conviction and commitment is not a part-time endeavor. <u>Consistency</u> is what makes them work. Consistency, which is defined as "the firmness of constitution or character," is what makes us better performers. It's also the "how" behind that betterment. It sends a message about your character. When it comes to your professional and personal goals, consistency is the difference between success and failure.

The June 2012 issue of *Inc.* magazine featured an interesting article about the power of consistency. It says following five important rules will make the difference between failure and success, and ensure *you* cross the finish line to achieving your goals. When it comes to conducting business, I believe these rules apply directly to service professionals. Here they are:

Rule #1 - Consistency allows for measurement

Measuring effectiveness in anything that you do it is important. If you are unable to measure your results, how can you decide whether to stay the course or change direction? The only way you can measure whether a relationship or something in your plan is effective is by working at it consistently—not by going at it like gangbusters for a week or two and then ignoring it for three. Your commitment has to be continuous over a period of time so you can monitor progress, register feedback, and determine if the activity is a success or failure.

Rule #2 - Consistency creates accountability

When you are accountable for your deliverables and goals, you're more likely to put a priority on spending regular time with your Level I's and to otherwise make yourself available to them. Your Level I's will appreciate the responsible behavior and leadership you display, which will motivate them to be more accountable to you. Being accountable to each other at your monthly meeting, by making sure you come prepared to discuss anyone and any situation that may be helpful to each other, is the catalyst that makes things happen.

Rule #3 - Consistency establishes your reputation

Having the conviction and the commitment to see things through by being consistent in your efforts will earn you a strong reputation. People who do the opposite and reinvent themselves each month—maybe by taking a "flypaper" approach to business and continually changing the markets and market segments they serve—will have a tough time establishing and keeping the relationships they need to get the referrals they want. "Identity shifters" like this really don't stand for anything, which causes their reputation and brand to be weak. Staying the course is a key factor in maintaining a strong mindshare position.

Rule #4 - Consistency makes you relevant

Your branding helps you differentiate yourself in a very crowded marketplace. Your branding activities are important for positioning you not only as an expert in your field, but as someone who is up on all the current issues surrounding it. The key to a successful branding campaign is to communicate this message effectively *and* consistently. Mindshare does not happen overnight. All too often, I've seen professionals get excited about sending their email broadcasts (containing helpful, relevant information), only to stop cold turkey after a few months because "other things" got in the way. The momentum they had just begun to create dissipated very quickly, as a useful branding strategy was abandoned. Please don't do this to yourself and your contacts. I encourage you to have a branding campaign that showcases your expertise and relevance. Most importantly, I implore you to stick with it!

Rule #5 - Consistency maintains your message

Your actions speak louder than words. Because of your deeply held conviction behind why you do what you do and your commitment to making a difference for others, the consistency of your message will always be intact. For those who do not have that conviction or the commitment, their intention becomes suspicious. People look at them and wonder, "What is real about this person, and what isn't? What is truth and what is fable?" If you consistently treat all people and situations with a high degree of importance, you gain a high level of trust. Your mindshare position, in turn, will always be strong.

Keeping The Shield Strong

No matter what stage of your career you're in—early, middle, or golden years—having the "Invincible Cs" gives you a great deal of protection against competitors who'd love to steal your mindshare position. Conviction, commitment, and consistency are a mighty trio that will help you build and sustain the business you want. Who wouldn't want to be in a Level I relationship with someone who has your conviction and commitment, and is always consistent in their actions? I hope you believe that you have the potential to strongly influence your Level I's through your leadership. By being dependably "all in" and giving the relationship 100% effort so there is mutual benefit, you will earn respect and admiration.

Your long-term plan has many aspects to it that are important. Having a strong belief in the plan you've created and a strong commitment to making it happen has spillover effects with regards to your relationship system. Specifically, your plan will dictate the type of people you choose to have in your relationship system. We have talked about the importance that consistency plays. **To achieve success, it is critical to keep the plan you built in Chapter 7 front and center at all times, and that you focus on consistently executing and progressing in all areas.**

Since perception is the overwhelming factor in people's decision whether to put you in a strong mindshare position, consistency in the way you **approach your personal goals is as equally important as the way you focus on your professional goals.** I know there will be times when it will be difficult to get out of bed and exercise the way you committed to when you wrote your plan. Strengthening your resolve might require you to have a bit of self-talk like this: *"If I get out and do the exercise I have committed to doing, I will continue to stay healthy, feel better and come across with a lot of energy today."* There is a reason you have goals in each section of your personal plan. They're meant to boost and support your well-being, so you can take on the challenges of work and home—and not only survive but thrive! So, be honest with yourself and ask, "With the conviction and commitment I have to achieving my plan, am I being consistent enough in my actions to make it happen?"

Practice Makes Perfect

In this chapter, we have looked closely at how "The Invincible C's" can protect your hard-earned mindshare position. What I don't want you thinking at this point is that you'll be great out of the chute if you have all the things we've talked about so far: a strong belief in yourself and in what you're doing for others, your commitment to that cause, and the willingness to stick with it to the end. **Yes, the C's are *necessary* for holding on to mindshare. But, they are not sufficient.** There is more...

Just like with Gary Player, the more you practice, the luckier you'll be in developing the relationships that will deliver the clients you want. The road to becoming a Navy SEAL, as we have learned, is incredibly hard. But, once someone achieves the designation, the learning doesn't stop—it just takes on an additional dimension. In a SEAL's line of work, lives are at stake and you must be able to perform flawlessly in extremely difficult circumstances. The only way a person can master that level of mental and physical demands is to practice, practice, practice. **You practice until what's required of you becomes second nature.**

In his book, *Outliers,* author Malcolm Gladwell says that it takes roughly 10,000 hours of practice to achieve mastery in any field. You might ask, "How does he arrive at that magical number?" and, "If it's true, will it actually take me that long to achieve success in my profession?"

In his search to find that answer, Gladwell studied the lives of extremely successful people in an attempt to learn how they achieved success. Were they born with a special talent? Or, were they just like you and me, but were willing to do what it took to be successful?

In *Outliers*, Gladwell shares a study done in the early 1990s by a team of psychologists in Berlin, Germany. The study looked at the practice habits of violin students. Specifically, the psychologists were interested in learning about the students' habits during childhood, adolescence and adulthood. Each of the subjects was asked, "Over the course of your entire career, ever since you first picked up the violin, how many hours have you practiced?" The study revealed that each of the violinists began playing at roughly five years of age, and practiced roughly the same number of hours.

Once they reached eight years of age, the number of hours began to diverge. By age twenty, the elite performers averaged more than 10,000 lifetime practice hours, while the less accomplished performers averaged less than 4,000 hours.

As a surprise by-product of the study, researchers learned that there were no "naturally gifted" performers who emerged among the elite violinists. In other words, contrary to what might have been expected, there were no violinists who achieved elite status *without* practicing 10,000 hours. Bottom line, the psychologists found a direct statistical relationship between hours of practice and achievement. There was nothing about being naturally gifted or taking shortcuts that would get a violin student to "master level" any faster!

Gladwell also shares the stories of the Beatles and Bill Gates, co-founder of Microsoft. People think that the Beatles were these four incredibly gifted musicians who were able to put songs together without effort and watch as they became instant hits. What people don't realize is that, in 1960, while they were still an unknown high school rock band, the Beatles went to Hamburg, Germany to play in local clubs for little or no money. **They did it because it gave them the opportunity to practice their craft.** Yes, they were underpaid and yes, they played in some terrible places with unappreciative audiences. So, why would anyone want to do that, you ask? Because, as young musicians just getting started, it gave the then unknown and inexperienced Beatles hours of playing time, which developed them as artists and helped transform them into world-class performers. Playing in front of audiences *forced* the Beatles to get better. As they established and polished their look and sound—and grew their brand—audiences demanded more performances. This, in turn, meant more playing time. By 1962, the Beatles were playing eight hours a night, seven nights a week. When they "suddenly" came on the international scene in 1964, it wasn't as if they had just started and became an instant success. The Beatles had already played over 1,200 concerts together! As a frame of reference, Gladwell reminds us that most bands don't play 1,200 times in their *career*!

The story of Bill Gates and the humble beginnings of Microsoft is similar. When you think about how large and dominant Microsoft is today, it's hard to believe that two college dropouts, Bill Gates and Paul Allen, could build a company of that size from the ground up (and become billionaires!). They must have been supremely gifted to pull off such a feat, right? Wrong. Yes, Gates and Allen were precocious and they loved mathematics. Those details are probably what got them to Lakeside School, an elite private school in the Seattle area. But Gates and Allen had thousands of hours of programming practice prior to founding Microsoft. They both joined the computer club at Lakeside School and became friends. The school purchased a computer terminal, which was significant in its own right. Terminals were rare back then (even at the university level), and this meant Gates had access to one in the eighth grade!

Gates and Allen quickly became addicted to programming. By the time he was a teenager, Gates was sneaking out of his house at night while his parents slept to do programming at nearby Washington University. Both Gates and Allen acquired their 10,000 hours of practice, so that when it came time to launch Microsoft in 1975, they were ready.

So, what does all this mean to you and what can you learn from it? **Simply this: If you want to be really good at what you do—including strengthening mindshare—you've got to**

be passionate about it and willing to work at it consistently. I don't question that you believe in yourself and have a strong conviction for what you do. But, so much of strengthening mindshare involves interacting with other people. So, it's important to get as good as you can at this skill.

And that means applying "The Invincible C's" and practicing building your relationships. Bear in mind that none of us will ever be experts at it, because every human being is different, based on his or her own orientation and experience.

Nevertheless, for the three C's to work for you, it's important that you are consistent about spending time with people and learning from those interactions. **If your social style is one where you enjoy sitting in your office doing the work without having to interact with other human beings, make it a point to get out and practice.** Practice until you become totally comfortable with people—that is, until it becomes second nature to you. Realize that, while you may find it difficult to relax, let alone enjoy, interacting with others right from the beginning that it will get easier and more rewarding—especially if you approach it with a positive attitude!

If you already enjoy being with people, practice being a better student of social styles. As we discussed in Chapter 6, **the better you can become at understanding how other people view the world, the greater "The Invincible C's" will work for you and help you maintain a strong mindshare position.**

As I have suggested, none of this will happen overnight. It's going to take time—quite possibly, more time than you'd like! Along those lines, let's take a look at two personal attributes that will play a huge role in helping you keep your mindshare position: patience and perseverance.

13

PATIENT PERSEVERANCE
It's A Marathon, Not A Sprint

"He that can have patience can have what he will"

—*BENJAMIN FRANKLIN*

Patience is a quality that is not very common in today's landscape. Our fast-paced, multi-tasking existence can make us feel like we're living at warp speed. Technology has helped us become very efficient and effective in many ways, but at the same time, has caused people to expect more and more from us sooner and sooner.

Add the need for speed to the hyper-competitive environment in which most of us operate, and it becomes even more difficult to be patient. We succumb to an "I want it now" mentality that bristles at the thought of standing in line or waiting in traffic. A lot of the road rage that occurs is caused by people who get impatient and end up totally disregarding others.

Since 2007, when the economy tanked, we have seen a significant increase in the number of professionals joining various networking groups. Why? Because jobs were on the line and people's incomes were at stake. The best way to stay employed was to become more valuable by drumming up business. Yes, many people in various disciplines lost their jobs. Were they the ones investing hours and hours networking, in hopes that someone would call them with a referral? Yes, but these were people who were forced to network because of the economic environment at the time. They really had nothing else to fall back on that would give them a more predictable stream of referrals. So, they did what they thought they had to do to take care of their families. Unfortunately, in many cases, their efforts weren't enough. Job loss even impacted partners who had been with firms for many years. Because they were on the servicing side (or, as I like to call it, the expense side) of the business, they became expendable.

There's no question that creating and sustaining a solid book of business with referral sources who hold you in their top mindshare position not only increases your value in the marketplace, but will provide you and your family the security you want for years to come.

As you well know, building a sustainable service business is not something that happens overnight. It takes what I call *patient perseverance*.

Patience is the ability to tolerate waiting for something worthwhile. **Perseverance** is the ability to stay the course despite the difficulties and challenges that occur along the way. It's having the tenacity to see things through because the goal is worthwhile. To exercise "patient perseverance," then, is to calmly work at your goal until you reach it.

There are some people who like networking because, even though they spend a lot of time doing it to little gain, networking requires no effort and can provide instant gratification—if you're lucky and somehow land a referral. **Many times, people network because they don't have an alternative strategy that will put them on a solid path to success.** Or, they're simply too impatient to make success happen.

I have been privileged to coach many fine professionals over the years. **While some gave up on their plan that we created together because they didn't want to do the work, the overwhelming majority stuck with their plan and reaped the benefits.** Have they had challenges along the way? No doubt. Did they question whether or not it made sense for them to continue? Absolutely. Doing something worthwhile is never easy—it just must be "worth the while," however long that may be.

Patient perseverance is not for the fainthearted. You have to really believe in what you're doing and know that there are going to be people and situations along the way that will try to make you quit. As we learned in the last chapter, your conviction must be strong. Because you're not getting continuous gratification, if you are not "all in" (fully believing in what you're doing), then there's a great possibility you might wave the white flag and surrender. For those who can get past those moments, the rewards can be significant.

The Patient Perseverance Of J. K. Rowling

J. K. Rowling, the author of the *Harry Potter* series, is a great example of what patient perseverance can mean. Rowling did not become a bestselling author (and one of the richest women in the world!) overnight. When she started writing her first book, she was penniless, recently divorced, and raising a young child alone. She wrote the first *Harry Potter* book on an old manual typewriter—a pretty incredible accomplishment for anyone.

Rowling was extremely proud of her manuscript and fervently knew that children as well as adults would enjoy *Harry Potter.* Unfortunately, the first publisher she took the book to gave her a resounding "No." While Rowling was very disappointed, she decided to press on and take the book to another publisher. Surely, they would publish it. The next publisher said "no" as well. I think you would agree it would've been easy at this point for Rowling to throw in the towel. But, because she believed in what she was doing, she took it to another publisher. They too said "no," followed by another and then another. Finally, on Rowling's thirteenth try, Barry Cunningham from Bloomsbury agreed to publish the book! Cunningham advised Rowling not to quit her day job, however, because he and other publishers "knew" there was no money to be made in children's books.

Boy, were they ever wrong! Today, *Harry Potter* stands as the best-selling book series and highest-grossing film series in history. And, because of her perseverance and patience in searching for someone who would believe in her story as much as she did, J. K. Rowling is a world-famous, award-winning author—and billionaire.

The Patient Perseverance Of Colonel Sanders

At age 65, Colonel Sanders, the founder of Kentucky Fried Chicken, witnessed the collapse of his expansive restaurant in Corbin, Kentucky. A new interstate highway killed his business when it lured travelers away from Route 25, the feeder for all his customers. When Sanders received his first Social Security check for $105, he decided he had two choices. The first was to complain bitterly that no one can live on $105 a month. Instinct told him no one would listen. His second choice was to find a way to create an income.

Sanders had developed a secret fried chicken recipe, made with 11 herbs and spices and a basic cooking technique that is still used today. He'd always received a lot of compliments on the chicken in his own restaurant, so he decided to offer the recipe to other restaurant owners to help them increase their sales. Sanders didn't ask for anything in return, other than 5% of the revenue generated by his secret-recipe chicken.

Sanders knew that if he spoke to enough restaurant owners that he would get the opportunity to help them sell more chicken. What Sanders did not realize is that calling on the owners would cause him to drive around the country for two years knocking on doors, sleeping in his car and wearing his famous white suit day in and day out. Do you know how many restaurant owners said "No" to Colonel Sanders before somebody said "Yes"? **Legend has it that it was 1,009 "no's."** Talk about perseverance! But, Sanders's patience and his belief in what his recipe could do for others paid off in the development of KFC franchisees across the country. When Sanders was 74, his chicken was being sold in 600 restaurants in the United States and Canada. He ended up selling his stake in KFC for $2,000,000.

The Patient Perseverance Of Walt Disney

The last story of perseverance I want to share with you is about Walt Disney. While the first two stories are pretty incredible, I find Disney's to be even more so, given he really had reason to doubt his abilities, yet went on to become an entrepreneurial and cultural icon. Believe it or not, Disney's first animation company went bankrupt and, incredibly, a news editor fired him because he "lacked imagination." Are you kidding me? While Disney enjoyed subsequent success with characters that he created—like Mickey Mouse, Pluto and Snow White and the seven dwarfs—he dreamed of building a clean, safe amusement park with attractions for parents and children to enjoy together. The idea started in 1940 and finally became reality on July 17, 1955, when Disneyland opened its doors. Legend has it Walt Disney was turned down over 300 times before he finally got the financing for his world-famous park. Today, Disney's incredible vision is delighting families from around the world. But, if it weren't for Disney's patience perseverance, no one would have ever experienced the fantasy world he imagined and was determined to see through to completion.

There are many other stories just like these three. What's the overriding theme? You can't enjoy success without failure. Michael Jordan once said, "I have missed 9,000 shots in my career. I have lost almost 300 games. On 126 occasions, I have been entrusted to take the game-winning shot, and I missed. I have failed over and over and over again in my life. And that is why I succeed."

You have invested heavily in your education and have taken the time and energy to learn the skills to be helpful to others. Why not be the best you can be? You have the ability within you! Realizing it comes down to how much you believe in what you're doing. **You are no different than J. K. Rowling, Colonel Sanders, or Walt Disney—really—if you are <u>passionate</u> about what you do and you <u>want to make a difference</u>.** If you follow the process and structure I have shared with you in this book and develop the right relationships to help others succeed, you will gain a powerful mindshare position—and deservedly so. But, also like Rowling, Sanders, and Disney encountered, there will be times when you're thrilled about your progress, and other times when you're discouraged by major bumps in the road. Those bumps will be challenges testing your resolve. If you are willing to patiently persevere, you will achieve your goals.

Benefits Of Developing Patience

There are many benefits to being patient. When you know what you're aiming for and that it will take time to hit your target, your stress levels come way down. You feel more in control.

Stress has a tendency to rear its ugly head when you believe "out there" is controlling you, when you don't have any direction, or when you feel like you don't have choices. Most people hope that success will come to them and that others will appear and give them what they want. In other words, rather than taking control of their lives, they let "out there" dictate whether they will be successful and happy.

Think about it: Can you make someone call and give you a referral? Can you predict who will call you and who won't? Most people spend a lot of time and energy focusing on the "if only." They tell themselves things like, "If only I had more referrals," or "If only my clients would refer me to other potential clients," or "If only there weren't so many people doing what I do, I could get more business," or "If only the economy were better," or "If only I had someone developing business so I could sit in the office and do the work." This is the self-talk of people who feel their lives are out of control. And, why do they feel out of control? Because they're not getting what they want. In fact, they may be making no progress towards achieving their goals at all. Instead, they end up wasting a lot of time venting and getting very little done.

Gary Applegate, Ph.D., a noted psychologist, author, and friend who wrote the book *Happiness: It's Your Choice: The Skill Development Theory for Developmental Change* says that the way for people to change from being problem solvers to what he calls "skill builders" is to think differently. So much of what we need to do is about taking the appropriate action. (On a related note, it's also important to recognize that, if you continue to do the same thing, you're going to get the same result.) The idea is to understand what you can and can't control—to take action where you can, and let the rest go. More specifically, Dr. Applegate says it's necessary to re-think what we have control over, what we have influence over, and what we can't control, and approach them accordingly.

You can only have patient perseverance when you feel in con-trol of your own needs. I know you want to be successful, to have a big book of business and to make a good income for you and your family. But to do that, Dr. Applegate says you must first assess five areas and rethink how things really are:

1. Rethink from "out there" to "me" to discover what you can control.

2. Rethink from a <u>want</u> level to a <u>need</u> level for fulfillment.

3. Rethink the notion of being forced, compelled, or victimized to seeing that you have choices.

4. Rethink being outcome-focused and instead learn to enjoy the process.

5. Rethink stress, which is really the difference between what you need and what you have, and realize you don't have to fear it! Realize that stress can also be an opportunity to help you grow.

On the journey to building the life you want for yourself and your family, you'd probably like to feel inspired and motivated, looking forward to each day instead of waking up feeling like you're on a perpetual hamster wheel trying hard to outrun all the wolves (like rent and other bills).

Well, you *can* have that kind of productive energy. The key is to feel like you have choices to meet your needs, so that you can enjoy not only a great business, but a happy life.

At this point, you probably accept that people have different personalities and orientations that cause us all to look at life a little differently. While we would often like people to move faster to help us get where we want to be, we can't approach them with an attitude of "I want to change you, so I can feel better by getting referrals from you NOW!" Dr. Applegate posits that, as adults, we tend to maximize our influence over others by coming across as being helpless or more powerful. He believes that we pay a big price for taking either position. Both require us to manipulate and control people, which is simply beyond our power.

You might want a recently converted Level I relationship, let's call him "Steve," to refer you a piece of business quickly, but Steve may not be willing or able to—which frustrates you. In this situation, you might not think you have a choice how to react, but you do. You can *choose* to feel stressed regarding Steve, because you haven't received the referral you **want** early in the Level I relationship. That would be a typical reaction. But, you don't have to react typically. **You have a choice: to simply react, or to rethink the situation.** Reacting will leave you feeling out of control and stressed. But by rethinking, you begin to look at the situation differently. It's just like the proverbial glass of water: some see it as half full, others as half empty. While the situation is the same, your interpretation of it depends on your orientation.

For example, what if you are able to help Steve be a better Level I for you by helping him increase his awareness of people and opportunities in his market and market segments? You can't control when Steve might send you a referral, but you can control caring about him—and demonstrating it (acting) by introducing him to people and potential situations that might help his business. These actions will influence Steve and, at some point, the universal law of reciprocity will come into play.

If others see that you enjoy working with them and going out of your way to help them, don't you think those actions will encourage them to find a way to help you? Dr. Applegate asserts that when you rethink your perceptions about relationships— from being something you use to get what you want to something that allows you to further the wants of others—ultimately, you will get what you want. It starts with the way you think. By rethinking situations you can control, instead of just reacting typically, and then taking action that centers on the other person's needs, you help create positive outcomes and feel gratified.

When you view your budding relationship system as an asset that appreciates over time and sustains a vibrant business, you will become more patient about what you are creating. I'm not sure who said, "Good things come to those who wait, but better things come to those who are patient," but I know they were on the right track! It's not about *waiting* to get favorable results. **I believe patience is about being in control of where you want to go and understanding what it will take to get there.** Patience says, "I understand that if I want to build a strong relationship system with 15 Level I relationships, I'm going to have to invest the time and effort for each of those relationships to be successful."

The important thing to remember is that you are investing your time on *your terms* in something that you know will be meaningful to you. If you decide you are unwilling to invest the time that is required to grow a reliable relationship system, you always have the choice not to do it. But, when you make the decision that you are going to do the work and that it will be a learning experience, complete with ups and downs, your patience will be rewarded.

Reading this book should help you understand that building the life you want is achievable. You will need to persevere. There's no question you will need to be patient. But you will also need to accept that you are dealing with human beings, some of whom may perform quickly in their Level I role, others who may take awhile before they can contribute to your success. We've agreed that you can't control people. **If you want the *relationship* to be successful, you will need to be committed—mentally and actually—to helping the other person be successful.**

There will be times when you're ready to throw in the towel. Patient Perseverance doesn't mean that you can't have those types of feelings on occasion. But, if you believe it's all worthwhile, you will get beyond those moments and keep moving forward. The alternative is to stop and give up.

Just like J.K. Rowling, Colonel Sanders, and Walt Disney, those who have conviction and commitment and consistently work to achieve their goals know there is no guarantee for success. But, they also know that if they stop, there is no chance of achieving the success they want. With a no-quit attitude and patient perseverance sustaining the relationship, you should have no trouble holding fast to your strong mindshare position for many years to come.

Wow! We've journeyed a long way together and looked at a number of different areas that provide opportunity to live the life you want. It's only fitting that we ride into the sunset together by looking at where it all starts and ends: with you!

14

IF IT IS TO BE, IT IS UP TO ME
Being Captain Of Your Ship

"Be the change you wish to see in the world."
—*GANDHI*

In this book, my goal has been to give you the benefit of my experience in coaching service professionals like you who work in highly competitive environments. I have shared with you both the quantitative and qualitative aspects of what it takes to get the referrals you want. I hope that I have made my case that you can attract the right referrals, while making your competition irrelevant. **But, it starts with you and your leadership.**

Everything that we have talked about only occurs when you provide the leadership to make it happen. Your success depends on others who believe in you and the willingness to take action. I do not want you to look back in that rearview mirror and say, "If only I had done this or done that."

Mother Teresa, who founded the Missionaries of Charity and dedicated her life to the poor and sick said it best: "Yesterday is gone. Tomorrow has not yet come. We have only today. Let us begin." She and those who served alongside her worked under very difficult conditions. Many of the people she cared for had lost hope, and much of what she did was to inspire them to live on.

I know that you are challenged each and every day. You are asked to be a leader in many areas of your life and also to take care of yourself so that you can continue to meet daily challenges. But here's what I also know: It all starts and ends with you. None of us can succeed by ourselves; we need each other. But *you* are the captain of your ship. You set the destination and chart the course. If you fail to reach that destination, you can't blame others, the economy, the demise of your specialty, or any other circumstance that got in the way of your being successful.

Do you really think people care if you're successful? I'm sure your family does. But, as far as others are concerned, the world goes on. If you don't succeed at something, someone else will. He or she will simply take what would have been your spot. It's as simple as that. If you want the brass ring, you have to be willing to go for it, full bore. Success is not linear—there are ups and downs. The key is to do the right things that will get you the right results.

Probably the most important benefit of being a service professional is that you get to control your life. You're not operating in a widget factory where you can't even go on break unless the whistle blows. You get to call your own shots. If you want a raise, you have the ability to go out and make that happen by acquiring more clients. If you want to rise to the top of your firm, you can. **You hold the power.**

If you are driving revenue to your firm, you never need to be concerned about the boss walking in your office with a big smile on his or her face to let you know that you've done a great job and have earned a paltry 2% or 3% raise for the next year. Instead, you will be in an esteemed position and well respected. On the flip-side, if you're not driving revenue, you're an expense and you serve at the need of your firm. And, as we all know, one of the objectives for companies and firms is to keep expenses as low as possible. So, as an "at will" employee, if the level of work falls, chances are you'll be moving on.

Like many professionals, you may have or are planning to have a family. That means you also have or want to have a nice home to raise your kids. With all that good stuff comes responsibility. Being able to put yourself into a position where you can create a lot of value for others and be rewarded for it is very exciting. It's not about working harder; it's about working smarter.

As we covered in earlier chapters, you could easily spend 20 to 30 hours a week attending networking events. Now, that's working "harder," because most events are in the evening and take time away from home life. But, I hope you agree at this point that it's definitely not working "smarter." Using time wisely is the mark of a good leader—which is how you must view yourself to be captain of your ship.

Taking the Lead

Leadership is such an important quality to have as a service professional because people enjoy working with and following a good leader. It's a critical component in your ability to create and maintain mindshare with your Level I's.

So, what constitutes leadership in the service professional's world? Let's take a look at some of the elements of leadership that are important and will help ensure you maintain a strong mindshare position.

Your Attitude

Everything starts and ends with your attitude. Why? Your attitude impacts everything else in your life. We all have a bad day from time to time. But those who live their life with a negative attitude will always find it difficult to maintain relationships—which, in itself, will have a negative impact on their career. Often, people like this have had a hurtful experience they can't move past and have allowed to define their lives. While others might feel compassion for these people, they will also avoid them like the plague, because they don't want negativity rubbing off on them.

As human beings, we are attracted to people who have a positive attitude. Positivity is something people *do* want to rub off on them—because it creates a feeling that good things will happen. We all want to be around someone who will make good things happen, right? Especially when things get tough. We know that positive people will be steady and that they will always find a way to get results. Having a positive attitude doesn't mean you have to have off-the-chart energy and excitement. I have known many amazing leaders whose DISC style was a C ("The Meticulous One") or S ("The Achiever"). They maintain an even keel to keep moving forward. Bill Gates, Alan Greenspan and Henry Kissinger all have the C social style. I don't think you would mistake them being for outgoing, gregarious people! However, their leadership style underscores a can-do attitude and a quiet confidence that motivates them to see things through, even in difficult times.

Leaders who have a positive attitude bring an energy that people can feel. When you live life as a positive person, your Level I's sense your energy (desire, accompanied by action) to build a mutually beneficial relationship. They feel your support and your encouraging thoughts and actions that will help them succeed. Your positive energy attracts other positive people, who approach things with the same energy. Just remember that, while positivity can be contagious, it doesn't happen automatically. <u>Choose</u> to be positive. Your leadership and enthusiasm will have an immense impact on those who become your Level I's—and even on service professionals and clients who are beyond your relationship system.

Principles of Leadership

Wess Roberts, Ph.D. and author of the acclaimed leadership book *Leadership Secrets of Attila The Hun* has a very interesting perspective on what leadership means:

> *"Leadership is the privilege to have the responsibility to direct the actions of others in carrying out the purposes of the organization, at varying levels of authority and with accountability for both successful and failed endeavors. It does not constitute a model or system. No model or system of leadership behaviors can anticipate the circumstances, conditions and situations in which the leader must influence the action of others."*

If you apply Roberts's take on leadership to your business as a service professional, you will find the issues are very similar to those faced by someone running a corporation or a private business. To thrive, a business requires leadership. As the owner, you are responsible for the results, whether good or bad. For you to be successful as a leader, you must be able to influence the actions of others.

My experience working with hundreds of service professionals shows that leadership is about being <u>supportive</u>. It is about being <u>collaborative</u>. It is about understanding that other service professionals are just like you. While they are working hard to build a great business, they too find it somewhat daunting. The positive energy and leadership you share with them in your Level I relationships will feel like a safe haven to them. And, it will engender trust and camaraderie.

In his book *Leaders Eat Last,* Simon Sinek points out that we have always been social animals. We do better working with others than trying to go it alone. He puts forth a strong argument that when we are part of a team or a group and trust the people we work with, we naturally work together to face any outside challenges and threats. When we try to do it alone or are "me"-focused, we are forced to invest our time and energy in protecting ourselves, because we're afraid that someone will want to take what we have, like a client or a referral source. Ironically, by going it alone, and with a mentality of scarcity, we increase our vulnerability to outside threats and challenges! Our myopic and fearful view blinds us to the opportunities that are available. **When we feel safe among the people we work with and approach them in a collaborative way, we are more likely to not only survive but thrive.**

Emptying the Teacup

The leadership you provide with the people in your relationship system and in other situations can be the difference between success and mediocrity (or even failure). It is not about your having all the answers and making all the decisions. Rather, it is about collaboration among service professionals, where both of you contribute and invest in the ideas and specific actions that will create mutual success. As a leader, it is important for you to be open-minded. Be intentional about listening to other people's ideas, no matter how different they may be from your own.

Have you ever heard the teacup story? It is a great visual for understanding what happens when we are not open to new ideas. Here is one version of it:

Once, a long time ago, there was a wise Zen master. People from far and near would seek his counsel and ask for his wisdom. Many would come and ask him to teach them, enlighten them in the way of Zen. He seldom turned any away.

One day an important man, a man used to command and obedience came to visit the master. "I have come today to ask you to teach me about Zen. Open my mind to enlightenment." The tone of the important man's voice was of one who was used to getting his own way.

The Zen master smiled and said that they should discuss the matter over a cup of tea. When the tea was served the master poured his visitor a cup. He poured and he poured and the tea rose to the rim and began to spill over the table and finally onto the robes of the wealthy man. Finally the visitor shouted, "Enough. You are spilling the tea all over. Can't you see the cup is full?"

The master stopped pouring and smiled at his guest. "You are like this tea cup, so full that nothing more can be added. Come back to me when the cup is empty. Come back to me with an empty mind."

Is your teacup full? If so, mentally empty it so that you are open to new ideas and ways to approach different issues in life. Even when you are in a leadership position, you must be open to learning—because once you stop learning, you stop being relevant. The benefit of being open to other people's ideas and opinions may mean the difference between your being good and becoming great.

Over the years, I have met some self-absorbed individuals. They were only interested in developing relationships that could give them something they couldn't get by themselves. Their minds were governed by the notion of scarcity, making it impossible for them to walk in someone else's shoes and understand their orientation. When you embrace and promote a spirit of selfless service to others to help them address their needs and desires, their trust in the relationship becomes very strong. As a result, they begin to freely give you their best to make the relationship mutually successful.

One of the best ways to boost people's confidence and increase their participation in the relationship is by not having all the answers. Asking questions and giving affirmations on ideas and the genius of others quickly elevates their confidence level, which makes them want to contribute to the success of the relationship. **Making it about them and not you is important.** Do not seek their adulation and don't become prideful. **Having an attitude of humility and caring is what will make the difference for you.** You want the other person to always feel that you are in this business-building endeavor together—and that together you will accomplish great things.

As you learned in the chapter on branding, regardless of your discipline, it's people's perception of you that matters. You are fighting for the number one position in the brain of another human being. A very small portion of what gets you there is related to the technical nature of—the utility—of what you do. Your utility merely gets you to the starting line. As a leader and the master of your fate, you have the ability to influence perception, especially when you work at it consistently. My goal for you as captain of your ship is that you go home each and every night feeling inspired, knowing that you had a great day, that you made a positive difference in someone's life, and that your brand became stronger as a result.

Making a difference in a referral source's life means that you value the relationship as more than just a conduit to a potential client and the fees that might generate. **Rather, you have a desire for that relationship to be mutually successful, and do everything you can to inspire and lead to ensure that eventuality.** You will show patience and persevere, even in the face of difficult and challenging issues that come into play. Your drive to succeed will carry you through.

Characteristics of Leadership

Jim Rohn, the famous entrepreneur, author and motivational speaker said that if you want to be a leader who attracts quality people, you must be a person of quality yourself. Leadership is an ongoing learning process that hinges on refining your skills. Rohn believed that all great leaders are constantly striving to improve their effectiveness. To up your effectiveness game, consider Rohn's seven personality traits of a great leader, and make them your own:

1. **Learn to be strong but not rude**. The people in your relationship system, your clients, and the other people along the way who will help you be successful will appreciate your being a strong leader. There is a difference between being strong and being rude. When you are rude, you

make it all about you. When you are strong, you make it all about those you touch and influence.

2. **Learn to be kind but not weak.** Some people equate kindness with weakness. But the people you touch, particularly those with whom you have a strong mindshare position, will appreciate your kindness. They will also appreciate that you are truthful and considerate. It's important that you be straightforward with people, but that you communicate in a way that is gentle and respectful.

3. **Learn to be bold but not a bully.** You operate in a very competitive marketplace and it is important that you be bold. You must be willing to put yourself out there without trying to be a hotshot or a bully. People need to know that you will do whatever it takes to help them be successful in the relationship and that you will deal with any problems that the two of you may encounter.

4. **You must learn to be humble but not timid.** Those who are timid in today's marketplace will be left behind. Having a sense of humility is not being timid. When you are humble, you put others first to help them succeed. It strengthens who you are as a person. Being timid, on the other hand, is being hesitant to take action. You will find that people respect humble leaders, and empathize with timid individuals—as they shake their heads and walk away (towards another referral source for their client).

5. **Be proud but not arrogant.** You take pride in your ambition and what you have accomplished thus far. You've worked hard and there's nothing wrong with giving

yourself a pat on the back now and then. But what's not okay is blurring the line between pride and arrogance. People who become arrogant tend to be very insecure. They often repel people who are genuine. Arrogance is almost like putting a shield around you that tells the "little people" they're unworthy of being in your presence. Now, why would anyone ever want that reputation? Unfortunately, some people wear arrogance like a badge of honor—they seem to confuse being snobby with commanding respect. Thankfully, they tend to be in the minority.

6. **Develop humor without folly.** As a leader, it's important to have a sense of humor. Since what you do every day is pretty serious business, bringing some levity into a relationship and helping both parties be more comfortable with each other is a good thing! Just be careful not to overdo it. As a leader, it's important that you aren't considered silly or foolish, which can make it difficult for people to take you seriously.

7. **Deal in realities.** Do your best to be 100% truthful. Your business and your life will not always be on a smooth highway. If you're working hard to make something happen, you're going to hit some nasty bumps in the road. Those bumps, however, can propel you to new heights! Just make it a point to be genuine with people. Regardless of the issues you're facing, don't put on a front and risk coming across as phony. I guarantee you; other people are often wrestling with the same problems. They know life has its ups and downs. And they will forgive you for not coming across as "perfect."

Your Mantra: If It Is To Be, It Is Up To Me

Based on what you've read in this chapter and everything that you've learned in this book, are you intrigued? Do I have your full attention? My hope is that I have inspired you to rethink what you can do to make a greater contribution to the world around you. Know that you are an amazing, unique human being. You have the ability to accomplish great things! The next time you are in a room full of other people, look around. You should realize there's not a single person there who is in any better position than you to take advantage of opportunities. Everyone gets dressed the same way you do. Everyone has similar responsibilities and challenges in their lives. Some of these people will succeed, some will get by, and some will fail.

How do people achieve success? By taking personal responsibility for their lives, mapping out a plan, and putting it into *action*. Whatever that plan will be, professional and personal, little steps to big steps, is entirely up to you. The tools presented in this book will accelerate your growth and confidence so you can plot your course and reach your destination. Your first commitment is to step aboard the ship.

When you create your three-year vision of where you want to take your business and your life, you will be excited. When you develop your first Level I relationship, you will feel more confident about where your business is going. When you start to exercise and begin to see some amazing results in how you feel and present yourself, you'll be overjoyed. When you can look back at the attention you were able to give those closest to you and how it impacted their lives, you will be tremendously satisfied. When you acquire a new hobby that gives you a lot of enjoyment and personal satisfaction, you will feel re-energized. When your brand has been developed and is strong, you will see its strength reflected in relationships where you hold the top mindshare position. When you have created the value for clients you have been referred to by your Level I relationships, you will see increased revenues and personal income for you and your family to enjoy. Finally, your hard work and success will allow you to enjoy the status you will hold in your firm, along with the admiration and respect of your colleagues.

It is all in your hands. And there is no better time than today to get started! The following is a fitting quote by self-help author and motivational speaker Wayne Dyer:

> *"There is no scarcity of opportunity to make a living at what you love; there's only scarcity of resolve to make it happen."*

Are you ready to put the secrets of mindshare to work for you? To make a successful living doing what you love as a service professional? I'm betting you are. When you put this book down, just stop for a few moments and think about everything you've learned. Envision yourself, your family, and the life you want. Now, say out loud:

> "This is my mantra that I will say each and every morning when I wake up and get to experience another great day on the journey to the success I want…
>
> If it is meant to be, it's up to me. As the captain of my ship, I choose the destination, I chart the course, and I commit to the journey, whatever it entails…"

Final Thoughts

It has been an incredible pleasure writing this book. Sitting down, reflecting on my nearly two decades as a business coach, and sharing my experiences with you on these pages so that you too will be able to enjoy the life you want has been truly satisfying. I hope you've found it an entertaining and useful read.

I'm grateful for the privilege of working with so many amazing people throughout my career. And, I'm proud to say that many who were willing to put in the effort and trust in themselves are still captaining their ship today. (Others are enjoying a happy and secure retirement.)

You can too.

My wish is that you now know what I know. Besides all the information I've provided in this book, you should *know* you can achieve the professional and personal success you desire. It's just up to you to believe in yourself and to use the secrets of mindshare to make it all happen.

HOW TO ACCESS PROGROWTH

1. If you would like to take advantage of managing your plan and relationship system within our online system tools, you may do so by going to www.progrowthpremier.com/mindshare.

2. When there, as a purchaser of the book, you can sign up and get 3 months free access.

3. Once you have your user ID and password, you will have access to the system. We will provide video instruction on how to use the system.

4. If you like using the tools and having access to our ongoing communication, you can continue to use the system for a nominal monthly fee after the end of your 3 month free access.

5. In addition, if you would like to take the DISC profile to determine your social style and how to use it as a strength, you may do it right on the site. As a purchaser of the book, you will pay a reduced fee when you sign up.

6. Any questions or issues, please contact us at ken@secretsofmindshare.com

About the Author

Ken Potalivo is the founder and CEO of ProGrowth, a professional coaching organization committed to helping people in service businesses succeed at work and at home. Ken started ProGrowth nearly two decades ago to address a problem faced by many bright people who have made huge investments in their education and skill development, yet struggle to achieve the success they desire.

He came to realize the solution lay in capturing attention: If potential clients would simply give these professionals a chance, they'd be won over by amazing service! In Secrets of MindShare, Ken shares everything he has learned and developed from working with hundreds of service professionals who have sought his guidance. The privilege of working with these men and the women and then witnessing their subsequent success is at the heart of his book.

Secrets of MindShare offers both quantitative and qualitative tools that will help the reader build a powerful brand—the very key to creating and sustaining mind share. As Ken explains, mind share holds the power to make your competition irrelevant and to get you the referrals you want.